P9-DFT-765

JOHN MARSHALL

SHOW ME THE
MONEY

**7
EXERCISES
THAT BUILD
ECONOMIC
STRENGTH**

Show Me the Money
© 2005 by John Marshall

John Marshall Enterprises
P.O. Box 159
Stone Mountain, Georgia 30086
(404) 286-1139
www.TheTeacher.us
jdm@johnmarshallenterprises.com
jm@TheTeacher.us

All rights reserved. No part of this book may be reproduced, stored in a retrieval system, or transmitted in any form or by any means without expressed written permission of the author.

Unless otherwise noted, Scripture verses are taken from the New American Standard Bible®, copyright © 1960, 1962, 1963, 1968, 1971, 1972, 1973, 1975, 1977, 1995 by The Lockman Foundation (www.lockman.org). Used by permission. Scriptures marked NLT taken from the Holy Bible, New Living Translation copyright © 1996 by Tyndale Charitable Trust. Used by permission of Tyndale House Publishers.

ISBN 0-9740693-7-X
Printed in USA
Cover design and layout: Cathleen Kwas

DEDICATION

I dedicate this book to my siblings. First is my baby sister, Dorothy "Dotty" Sue Marshall, who has been the central focus of our family for more than forty-five years. When she was just a toddler, an inappropriate medical prescription permanently damaged some brain cells and she has been mentally challenged since then. However, through her we have learned to exercise great patience and diligent care.

Next, I dedicate this book to my older sister, Gladys Marshall McGowan. Thank you for believing in me and continually encouraging me to reach for greater heights. Your tender loving care for Daddy while he was deteriorating and even now for Mommy as she grows older will never be forgotten. Thanks for positioning yourself front and center and being the strong woman that you are.

Also, I dedicate this book to my older brother, Clarence Marshall. During our childhood and early adolescent, I know that you wondered many times if I would ever grow up and stop pestering you and the older boys whom I could not whip. You are demonstrating that one can rise, fall, and rise again. Thanks for the lessons I have learned.

Last but not least, I dedicate this book posthumously to my oldest brother, John L. Boyd. You always "wondered out loud" the source of my finances. Now you know. Though you were the oldest, you came into our life latest, but, oh, what a joyful reunion it was. Thanks for the memories and even the unfinished promises that you made two days before the tragic accident that took you away. Rest in peace; I have done my best to honor them for you.

ACKNOWLEDGMENTS

No person lives on an island alone. Every product owes its production to numerous influences. That is certainly true of my writings. Long before I ever thought about writing, I was being prepared unknowingly for just such a challenging task.

There was the theological influence. I remember hearing the crystal-clear voice of Walter H. Vance each Sunday morning over radio station WTJS in Jackson, Tennessee, as he spoke on "Search the Scriptures" frequently saying, "You are teaching things the apostles never taught." Also, I remember waiting with anticipation for the theme song, *That We Might All Be One*, to conclude so that we could hear the booming voice of Nokomis Yeldell coming over WDIA radio station in Memphis, Tennessee. Ultimately, having the privilege to engage in a three-hour textual study of the Holy Scriptures with Ben Thomas Adams proved to be most rewarding.

There was the intellectual influence. Frequently, my high school history teacher, Mr. Roscoe Burton, would say, "Marshall, come here. Try to be intelligent. Anyone can be ignorant." Later, there were many Monday mornings when I would arrive at work to find on my desk a copy of my newspaper column that had appeared the previous Saturday in *The Jonesboro Sun*. My coworker, Calaria G. Cage, had grammatically critiqued every word. Even the torturous experiences of reading those critiques proved to be helpful. Pointed challenges and charges go a mighty long way.

There was the practical influence. Ada Day Allen, you were the first person to verbalize the potential redemptive value in my writing. After almost fifteen years, I have begun to write the book that you first suggested. Diana Scimone, I could not have done it without your help. You restructured the dangling participles into helpful principles.

To all I say, "Thanks." You have completed a job "well done." I will now strive to hold up my end of the franchise.

TABLE OF CONTENTS

Chapter 1

HOW DID WE GET IN THIS MESS?

I once had the privilege of working for someone who was extremely wealthy. In fact, he was the richest man in the town where I lived. He was probably fifteen or twenty times richer than anybody in the town. I worked for him when I was twenty-two years old, and I used to watch him carefully. I watched the entire family. This man worked long hours. He owned twenty-seven auto parts stores. His sons were single and millionaires, and could have driven any car they wanted. One of them rode in a Ford F-150 custom pick-up truck, and the others drove Datsun B-210 hatchbacks.

I was amazed at how conservative they were. The father would fuss at his son because he found a screw on the floor. I heard him say, "That's three cents we're wasting."

Now, I was pretty poor, and I watched how this family handled their business and their finances. If this man needed to pay attention to a three-cent screw lying on the floor, I knew I had to pay attention to what I had. If he got where he was by accounting for every three-cent screw, I needed to do the same.

In the years since that job, I have learned many things about finances. I have learned that money is like morphine. When used wisely, it reduces much pain. When used unwisely, it creates much pain. Finances—and the way we use them—can bring us stress or stability or strength. My goal in this book is to help us develop a plan to move from financial stress to financial stability to financial strength.

Let us begin by looking honestly at where we are. According to Dr. Kregg Hood in the leader's guide for his book *Escape the Debt Trap*, we are in financial turmoil. He reminds us that many people today are suffering financial stress. Credit debt is at an all-time high, and savings at an all-time low. Hood says that in the United States, the average credit-card debt per family is $8,367, and that half of all credit-card holders report difficulty in making their minimum payments. Last year, forty percent of Americans spent more than they earned. Financial crisis is the number one cause of divorce.[1]

---

[1] *Escape the Debt Trap*, by Dr. Kregg Hood (Prime Source Providers), page 2; www.escapethedebttrap.com

How did we get this way? I can think of at least three reasons: impulsive indulgence, impulsive impatience, and impulsive inaccuracy.

IMPULSIVE INDULGENCE

Naboth owned a vineyard that bordered the property of King Ahab, the husband of Jezebel.

> Now it came about after these things that Naboth the Jezreelite had a vineyard which was in Jezreel beside the palace of Ahab king of Samaria. Ahab spoke to Naboth, saying, "Give me your vineyard, that I may have it for a vegetable garden because it is close beside my house, and I will give you a better vineyard than it in its place; if you like, I will give you the price of it in money" (1 Kings 21:1-2).

It sounded like a good deal, but there only one problem. God forbade the inheritance of the sons of Israel to be transferred from one tribe to another (see Numbers 36:7, Leviticus 25:23). Although King Ahab could financially afford to buy the land, Naboth could not rightfully sell it, so he refused. King Ahab went home, lay on his bed, and pouted. After his wife, Jezebel, determined the cause of his misery, she reminded him that he was the king, and therefore should have his heart's desire. She devised a treacherous scheme to kill

Naboth and steal his vineyard, but after this dirty deed had been done, the prophet Elijah brought a word from the Lord. God brought death to Jezebel and much evil upon King Ahab in subsequent generations (see 1 Kings 21:4-29).

Ahab and Jezebel's pain came through their attitude of impulsive indulgence, which says, "I have to buy everything that I want." This attitude of "I gotta have it" leads to economic discontent, which in turn leads to ruin. This attitude, of course, did not die when Ahab and Jezebel died. It continues to withhold economic contentment from many as they move from one income level to another. A person making $50,000 a year begins to make $60,000. Shortly before they receive their wage increase, they begin to spend at the $60,000 level. Why would they do this? They really believe, "I should buy all that I can buy." It is the attitude of impulsive indulgence, and it opposes the development of a financial cushion called savings.

It is sad that after someone has received a wage increase, he or she begins to use more credit than before. It seems logical that a child who received a $100 per month allowance while in college should be able to save $500 per week of their $1,000 per week salary the month after graduation. After all, they would still have $1,900 more to spend than a month earlier—but the attitude of "I gotta have it" rushes in alongside the credit cards. How unfortunate.

A wife who was not working for a period of time begins to earn $1,000 per week. Shouldn't she be able to save $500 per week? After all, she has $500 per week more to spend than she previously had, but the attitude of "I gotta have it" rushes in alongside the new credit cards that she and her husband apply for. How sad.

I once conducted a premarital preparation session for a prospective bride and groom who were already in debt. They each rented their own apartment. Her rent and utilities amounted to $1,087.30 per month, while his were slightly more. I suggested that after they married, the bride should move from her one-bedroom apartment to his one-bedroom apartment, rather than both of them moving into a new and larger place. By doing so, they could reduce their expenses by the total cost of her apartment, $1,087.30 per month, resulting in a savings of $13,047.60 in one year. I also pointed out how this savings could erase all their indebtedness or serve as a down payment on their first house.

The prospective bride squirmed at this suggestion, and when she could contain herself no longer, she blurted out, "I have waited this long to get married. I am certainly not going to sacrifice in a small apartment any longer. We are going today to put a deposit on a three-bedroom condo." To some degree, this attitude plagues many newlywed couples. The bride-to-be expects to improve her standard of living immediately when the marriage takes place. And the attitude of "I gotta have it" continues to plague our society. In the coming chapters, we will look at numerous ways to arrest this attitude.

IMPULSIVE IMPATIENCE

Impulsive indulgence says, "I gotta have it," but impulsive impatience says, "I gotta have it now." Jesus taught His disciples to stop worrying about their financial and economic standing. He reminded them how God takes care of the birds. Since His disciples are more valuable than birds, certainly God will take care of them (see Luke 12:22-32). What father would feed the chickens and starve the children?

Jesus taught His disciples to stop worrying about their financial and economic standing.

Creative advertising sparks an attitude with many consumers that leads to their financial ruin. Advertising ignites the attitude of impulsive impatience, which says "I gotta have it now." The children of Israel, God's chosen people, left Egypt on their way toward the Promised Land. Moses had died and God had crowned Joshua as their new leader (see Joshua 1:2). God renewed His promises to Joshua, reminding him that He would favor him just as He had promised to favor Moses:

> "Every place on which the sole of your foot treads, I have given it to you, just as I spoke to Moses. From the wilderness and this Lebanon, even as far as the great river, the river Euphrates, all the land of the Hittites, and as far as the Great Sea toward the setting of the sun will be your territory. No man will be able to stand before you all the days of your life Just as I have been with Moses, I will be with you; I will not fail you or forsake you. Be strong and courageous, for you shall give this people possession of the land which I swore to their fathers to give them. Only be strong and very courageous; be careful to do according to all the law which Moses My servant commanded you; do not turn from it to the right or to the left, so that you may have success wherever you go. This book of the law shall not depart from your mouth, but you shall meditate on it day and night, so that you may be careful to do according to all that is written in it; for then you will make your way prosperous, and then you will have success. Have I not commanded you? Be strong and courageous! Do not tremble or be dismayed, for the Lord your God is with you wherever you go" (Joshua 1:3-9).

ed them success and prosperity right before
ie city of Jericho. Jericho stood between them
sed Land. God reminded them that the items
ty of Jericho were under a curse and that all
belonged to the Lord. He warned them not to covet those
items, but to spare only Rahab and her household. The silver
and gold articles were to go into the treasury of the Lord.
They were not to take them for their personal collections.

The temptation proved too great for Achan. He could not
resist, and stole what God had told him to leave alone. The
next day, the Israelites went to battle against the city of Ai.
Because of Achan's misdeeds, God withdrew His favor from
them, thirty-six people died in battle, and Israel was defeated.
Achan had the stolen items in his tent, but not the favor of
God on his team. Which was more valuable? Achan's attitude
of impulsive impatience caused him not to wait for God to
prosper him; instead, he attempted to take what God had
forbidden. God ordered Achan to be stoned. His attitude of "I
gotta have it now" led to his total ruin. Likely, we know
people who have suffered similar fate.

I am not suggesting we take an oath of poverty. I am saying
that as we climb the economic ladder, we should be
content—content with little while we are healthily working
toward much.

Not that I speak from want, for I have learned to be content in whatever circumstances I am. I know how to get along with humble means, and I also know how to live in prosperity; in any and every circumstance I have learned the secret of being filled and going hungry, both of having abundance and suffering need. I can do all things through Him who strengthens me (Philippians 4:11-13).

Economic contentment means keeping our priorities in line. The attitude of impulsive impatience, on the other hand, causes us to ignore priorities. We can look at the example of the Israelites who had been captured, deported to Babylon, and now allowed to return to Jerusalem. The people of Haggai's day had built and beautified their own houses, yet the temple, the house of God, was incomplete. The people reasoned, "The time has not come, even the time for the house of the Lord to be rebuilt" (Haggai 1:2), but the real problem was that they had reversed their priorities. Haggai reminded them of their wrong priorities:

Then the word of the Lord came by Haggai the prophet, saying, "Is it time for you yourselves to dwell in your paneled houses while this house lies desolate?" Now therefore, thus says the Lord of hosts, "Consider your ways! You have sown much, but harvest little; you eat, but there is not enough to be satisfied; you drink, but there is not enough to become drunk; you put on clothing, but no one is warm enough; and he who earns, earns wages to put into a purse with holes" (Haggai 1:3-6).

God has always wanted His people to take care of Him first, and then He would take care of them. That was the principle of the "first-fruits" offering (see Exodus 23:15-19). Jesus even underscored that concept when He challenged His disciples to seek first the kingdom of heaven (see Matthew 6:33).

An attitude of impulsive impatience will cause us to ignore not only priorities, but also price. Jesus said:

> "For which one of you, when he wants to build a tower, does not first sit down and calculate the cost to see if he has enough to complete it? Otherwise, when he has laid a foundation and is not able to finish, all who observe it begin to ridicule him, saying, 'This man began to build and was not able to finish'" (Luke 14:28-30).

Some things just cost too much. Everything is bound to go on sale at some point in time. Rather than asking, "Is the price reasonable" or "Do I really need this?" this attitude will cause us to ask "Where do I sign?"

How can we deal with the attitude of impulsive impatience? We will answer that question in coming chapters.

IMPULSIVE INACCURACY

The attitude of impulsive inaccuracy says, "I gotta have it now, but I do not know what I have to get it with." This very dangerous attitude will lead to our economic ruin. The notion that "the less I know about my resources, the better I will be" is absurd, yet it lodges in the consciousness of many adults. Instead of leading to economic contentment, it leads to economic discontent.

Impulsive inaccuracy says, "I gotta have it now, but I do not know what I have!" The notion of "the less I know about my resources, the better I will be" rapidly leads to ruin. Jesus knew what He had before He fed the multitudes (see John chapter 6). Joseph knew what he had before the famine in Egypt (see Genesis chapter 41). The Levites knew what they had after they repaired the temple and used it to make more utensils for the house of the Lord (see 2 Chronicles chapter 24). Impulsive inaccuracy, however, says that this type of accounting is not needed before or after a project. It will quickly lead to ruin, as many have discovered.

How do we counteract these dangerous and destructive attitudes? Keep reading! In the coming pages, we will learn about God's economic system (and how it is very different from ours) and the privileges given to those who are part of it. We will reveal seven exercises that will help us to take control of our finances and experience financial freedom.

And we will develop a plan to teach these principles to our children and our children's children.

If impulsive indulgence, impatience, and inaccuracy are all too familiar, then we must make a decision today to ask God to help us understand and apply His principles outlined in this book. If debt and bad financial attitudes have kept us in bondage for too long, the time has come to break those chains. Please notice that the subtitle of this book is not "seven easy exercises." The steps we must take to gain financial control and freedom are not easy, and there will be points as you read this book that you may want to throw it away and head for the mall—but I encourage you to press on. The joy and peace awaiting us when we are financially strong far surpass anything we can buy at the mall, computer store, or new car showroom.

It begins with the decision to move from financial stress to financial stability. A good feeling will rush through us when we go to the mail box, receive our bills, and are able to pay them the day they come in. God does not want us to take the bills home and stress over them. Then, we must make the decision to move from financial stability to financial strength. God wants His people to have enough financial strength and muscle to be able to make an impact in the world for His Kingdom! After we have moved from financial stress to financial strength, we can (and should) reach back and help somebody else to make the same journey.

Ready to make the move from financial stress to financial stability to financial strength? Let us begin.

THOUGHT PROVOKERS

1. How has financial stress affected your life? Your marriage? Your children?

2. What percentage of last year's income can you account for? Last month? Last week? Can you say what percentage of your money went for food? Clothing? Utilities? Luxuries? Non-luxury items?

3. Are you serious about making the move from financial stress to financial stability to financial strength? Do you think there will be obstacles on the path? How can you prepare to deal with them?

Chapter 2

WHAT IS MONEY?

Several years ago, James Peterson and Peter Kim co-authored a book entitled *The Day America Told the Truth*, reporting on the results of a survey taken of thousands of people. The authors promised anonymity to the survey respondents. One of the questions was, "What would you be willing to do for $10,000,000?"

We can take a moment to think about what our answer would be. If no one would ever know who we were or what we did, what would we do for $10,000,000? According to the survey, seven percent of the respondents said they would murder an absolute stranger for that sum of money. Twenty-three percent said they would work as a prostitute for one week. Five percent said they would abandon their families, including their husband or wife, their children, and even their parents.

What does that say to us about the tremendous influence of money? Money exercises influential powers. It creates and changes thought processes. Also, it causes people to do what they otherwise would never do.

Today many people use money to define who they are. We must never define ourselves in terms of what we have. We must never allow others to define us in terms of what they think we should have. Money is simply a means of assigning value and transferring value from one person to another and from one place to another.

Hundreds of years ago, people exchanged labor and/or traded resources (or products) to obtain the things they wanted or needed. For example, a person might exchange a day's work for 100 pounds of beef. Another person might exchange two dozen eggs for one pound of sugar. When the people and products were few, this barter system worked well. However, as population and products increased, the barter system became impractical. In its place, society developed a "monetary" system. Money became a means of assigning value and transferring value from one person to another and from one place to another. Products and services were assigned a monetary value making it easier to transfer from one person to another and from one place to another. Value representation and value transference were the purposes of money.

We should never, however, praise poverty nor demonize wealth.

This system is in operation today—whether on the international level, national level, or family level. When parents give $5 to their child, the child increases his or her worth by $5, and the parents' worth decreases by $5.

We can be a whole person whether or not we have any money. We can be a healthy person whether or not we have any money. We were whole when we came into the world, and we came without money. We can be whole and healthy when we leave this world. We will come and go without money. "For we have brought nothing into the world, so we cannot take anything out of it either" (1 Timothy 6:7).

We should never, however, praise poverty nor demonize wealth. God has always used the rich—men and women such as Adam, Abraham, Solomon, Esther, and others. It is fine to legitimately obtain more than just the bare necessities. We should not feel guilty when we begin to acquire a lot of money, but we must remember that we were complete before and we can be complete after.

WHAT IS MORE VALUABLE THAN MONEY?

Solomon, the son of David, was charged with being king over all of Israel (see 2 Chronicles 1:8-12). Solomon recognized his deficiency, and prayed that God would give him the wisdom necessary to lead the people of God. God blessed him with more than adequate wisdom for the job. In fact, Solomon became the wisest man who ever lived. In addition to wisdom, God granted him wealth beyond the wealth that any other person had ever enjoyed. Solomon became the wealthiest and the wisest person who ever lived.

We should never expect money alone to make us happy. Likely, our yearnings will always exceed our earnings. Many have enjoyed financial income beyond their dreams, yet to their dismay, great sums of money did not automatically bring a greater level of happiness. Satan leads people to believe that if they were in a different set of circumstances they would auto-matically be happier. Do we really think if we had the job that someone else has, the house that someone else has, or even the spouse that someone else has that we would be happier?

Solomon experienced it all, and we can gain from his experiences. He learned the futility of worry, and therefore he counseled, "Do not weary yourself to gain wealth, cease from your consideration of it" (Proverbs 23:4). Pursuing wealth has frustrated many, especially those who spend their every waking moment dreaming of wealth. Those who set their hearts on wealth and run after it soon notice how slippery it can be. "When you set your eyes on it, it is gone. For wealth certainly makes itself wings like an eagle that flies toward the heavens" (Proverbs 23:5).

The apostle Paul gave his protégé, Timothy, similar advice: "Instruct those who are rich in this present world not to be conceited or to fix their hope on the uncertainty of riches, but on God, who richly supplies us with all things to enjoy" (1 Timothy 6:17). Millions have committed economic suicide because they failed to heed this advice. After pursuing wealth, their life turned worse than ever before.

I am not suggesting that being poor is a virtue within itself. However, I am saying that the idea of having wealth alone does not automatically provide a greater level of happiness. After Solomon had experienced all that he dreamed, he concluded that all was folly (see Ecclesiastes 2:4-11). In 1992, while reading for a research paper at the University of Memphis, I discovered the interesting fact that the highest rate of suicide was among rich elderly Caucasian men, while the lowest rate was among poor elderly Negroid women. At that time, research also indicated that a direct correlation existed between dependency upon God and suicide. Those who were most likely to depend upon God were least likely to commit suicide. Those who were least likely to depend upon God were most likely to commit suicide.

When King Solomon asked God to give him knowledge and wisdom, this was God's reply:

> "Because you had this in mind, and did not ask for riches, wealth or honor, or the life of those who hate you, nor have you even asked for long life, but you have asked for yourself wisdom and knowledge that you may rule My people over whom I have made you king, wisdom and knowledge have been granted to you. And I will give you riches and wealth and honor, such as none of the kings who were before you has possessed nor those who will come after you" (2 Chronicles 1:11-12).

Solomon received wisdom and wealth, and throughout the book of Proverbs, he shares much of his wisdom. We would be wise to read and learn from the wisest and wealthiest man of his day. In fact, we have opportunities above those that Charles Schwab and E. F. Hutton offer.

According to Solomon, some things are more valuable than money. Money is necessary as a medium of exchange. In order to leave Kroger with groceries, we need money. It is a medium of exchange, yet some things are more valuable than money. Solomon says that righteousness and integrity are more valuable than money. "He who profits illicitly troubles his own house, but he who hates bribes will live" (Proverbs 15:27). Illicitly gained money confuses our house. Again,

Solomon said, "Better is a little with righteousness than great income with injustice" (Proverbs 16:8). It is far better to have a little and maintain our righteousness than to be guilty of the injustice of receiving a great gain. Time and time again, Solomon warned against illicit gain. "Better is a poor man who walks in his integrity than he who is perverse in speech and is a fool…What is desirable in a man is his kindness, and it is better to be a poor man than a liar" (Proverbs 19:1, 22). "A good name is to be more desired than great wealth, favor is better than silver and gold" (Proverbs 22:1). Forever abandon the notion that "I should get all that I can get at any cost."

Solomon also said that peace and love are more valuable than money. Evaluate the profundity of his words: "Better is a little with the fear of the Lord than great treasure and turmoil with it. Better is a dish of vegetables where love is than a fattened ox served with hatred" (Proverbs 15:16-17). "Better is a dry morsel and quietness with it than a house full of feasting with strife" (Proverbs 17:1).

The contentment of peace and love is a priceless commodity that is much more valuable than money. Some things are above the price of money. Whereas money as a medium of exchange purchases the necessities of life, there are some things that money cannot buy. Some things are simply not for sale. Nothing is free, but all is not for sale. The best things in life may not be free, but they cannot be bought with money. Money, for example, cannot provide safety and security. No matter how many padlocks we purchase, safety and security are not for sale.

Solomon understood how the human mind enjoys deception. Often what we believe provides security in fact provides only within our imagination. Solomon said, "A rich man's wealth is his strong city, and like a high wall in his own imagination" (Proverbs 18:11). Only within his imagination is the rich man safe. We cannot operate all day long within the protective environment of our imagination. If we really knew how vulnerable our security system was, we probably would refuse to purchase it. Of course, some things do increase the probability of safety, yet at best much is still desired.

Solomon warned, "Do not weary yourself to gain wealth, cease from your consideration of it. When you set your eyes on it, it is gone. For wealth certainly makes itself wings like an eagle that flies toward the heavens" (Proverbs 23:4-5). Wealth is like an eagle and it will fly away on its own and we cannot retrieve it.

In 1926, ten of the world's wealthiest men attended a meeting in New York City—yet years later, all ten of these once-wealthy men died broke. Their money took flight and flew away. Money cannot buy safety and security.

Nor can it provide permanency and salvation. "Riches do not profit in the day of wrath, but righteousness delivers from death" (Proverbs 11:4). "The righteousness of the upright will deliver them, but the treacherous will be caught by their own greed...He who trusts in his riches will fall, but the righteous will flourish like the green leaf" (Proverbs 11:6, 28).

If we have sold our righteousness and integrity, what did we get for it? What do we now have of value that we received because we compromised our standard of righteousness and integrity? Can we repurchase our righteousness and integrity with the proceeds from our sale? Never. Never. Never. It was a bad deal.

God gives us another warning: "Instruct those who are rich in this present world not to be conceited or to fix their hope on the uncertainty of riches, but on God, who richly supplies us with all things to enjoy" (1 Timothy 6:17). The apostle Paul wrote these words to the preacher Timothy in order to instruct him what to teach members of the church. His words are a warning not to fix our hope on the uncertainty of wealth. King Solomon knew this all along. Rather than trusting wealth, we should trust and fix our hope in God. He not only supplies, but richly supplies.

THOUGHT PROVOKERS

1. How did your understanding of money change after you studied this chapter?

2. How do you react to this statement: "God is the only perma-
nent, stable force"? How do you react to this Scripture verse:
"Instruct them to do good, to be rich in good works, to be
generous and ready to share" (1 Timothy 6:18)?

3. Where is your hope? In whom (or what) is your confidence? When you trust God, how do you react when the
stock market fluctuates? What happens when your investments go south?

Chapter 3

WAS JESUS POOR?

O ur financial attitudes yeserday have likely determined our financial altitudes today. Here are some common statements uttered yesterday that can determine our financial altitudes today:

"I have so many bills that I'm never going to be able to pay all of them."

"I have been poor all my life. I was born poor, I am now living poor, and I will just die poor."

Some people who think and talk like this have even increased their financial indebtedness because they were anticipating bankruptcy. After filing bankruptcy, they return to the same financial lot as before. Why? Their attitude towards finances created their actions toward money, which determined their altitude with money.

Among these misguided individuals stand many believers. True believers must abandon these false notions. True believers should look forward to paying their debts, getting out of debt, and enjoying life. If Jesus remains as our model, we will be well on our way.

...if Jesus became poor, there must have been a point in time when He was not poor.

WHEN JESUS BECAME POOR

Was Jesus poor? No, but the Bible teaches us that He *became* poor: "For you know the grace of our Lord Jesus Christ, that though He was rich, yet for your sake He became poor, so that you through His poverty might become rich" (2 Corinthians 8:9). Notice that the text clearly says Jesus *became* poor. It does not say that He *was* poor. So if Jesus *became* poor, there must have been a point in time when He was not poor. Knowing when He was not poor will help us to better understand the financial strength of Jesus. Understanding the financial strength of Jesus will not only challenge our attitude toward our personal finances, but also revolutionize it. And revolutionizing our attitude about money will likely revolutionize our financial aptitude and altitude.

In order to show that Jesus was not poor, let's look at some of the ways that Jesus behaved. The people whom Jesus hired indicate that He was not poor. Jesus hired twelve full-time ministry workers.

> Jesus summoned His twelve disciples and gave them authority over unclean spirits, to cast them out, and to heal every kind of disease and every kind of sickness. Now the names of the twelve apostles are these: The first, Simon, who is called Peter, and Andrew his brother; and James the son of Zebedee, and John his brother; Philip and Bartholomew; Thomas and Matthew the tax collector; James the son of Alphaeus, and Thaddaeus; Simon the Zealot, and Judas Iscariot, the one who betrayed Him. These twelve Jesus sent out after instructing them: "Do not go in the way of the Gentiles, and do not enter any city of the Samaritans; but rather go to the lost sheep of the house of Israel. And as you go, preach, saying, 'The kingdom of heaven is at hand.' Heal the sick, raise the dead, cleanse the lepers, cast

out demons. Freely you received, freely give" (Matthew 10:1-8).

Jesus hired these twelve apostles and sent them out to do ministry. Can we afford twelve families? If not, then likely Jesus was wealthier than we are. How many people can afford the salary of twelve people? Not many. Very likely, Jesus was wealthier than most.

Jesus not only did not send them out as beggars (consumers), but He told them to give freely. How could they freely give? They had freely received. Jesus gave to them and expected them to give to others—and He did not stop there. In addition to hiring twelve full-time ministry workers, Jesus hired seventy additional workers. "Now after this the Lord appointed seventy others, and sent them in pairs ahead of Him to every city and place where He Himself was going to come" (Luke 10:1). Can we afford to hire seventy families? If not, then likely Jesus was wealthier than we are. How many people can afford the salary of seventy people? Not many. Very likely, Jesus was wealthier than most.

There are other indications that He was not poor. Jesus had a treasury, a money box, "Now he [Judas] said this, not because he was concerned about the poor, but because he was a thief, and as he had the money box, he used to pilfer what was put into it" (John 12:6). Who, other than the wealthy, have a treasury? Not only did Jesus have a treasury, but He also had a treasurer, Judas. Who, other than the wealthy, have need of a treasurer?

Jesus had a thief as His treasurer. The word *pilfer* is trans-lated from the Greek word *klepta,* from which we get our English word *kleptomaniac,* which means that Judas was not a one-time thief; he was a regular thief. Judas stole from the treasury on a regular basis—yet there remained enough money to support eighty-two families. Now imagine that. Jesus had enough money in His treasury to hire ministry workers and pay them, even though His treasurer was regu-larly stealing from the treasury.

What Jesus gave indicates that He was not poor. While Jesus ate with His disciples, He had a private conversation with Judas that either the other disciples did not hear or simply did not hear well enough to understand, for Simon Peter questioned Jesus about the one who would betray Him (see John 13:21-25). Jesus responded to Simon's question:

> "That is the one for whom I shall dip the morsel and give it to him." So when He had dipped the morsel, He took and gave it to Judas, the son of Simon Iscariot. After the morsel, Satan then entered into him. Therefore Jesus said to him, "What you do, do quickly." Now no one of those reclining at the table knew for what purpose He had said this to him. For some were supposing,

because Judas had the money box, that Jesus was saying to him, "Buy the things we have need of for the feast"; or else, that he should give something to the poor (John 13:26-29).

When Judas suddenly left to commune with those to whom he would shortly betray Jesus, the other disciples thought he was going to purchase things for the feast or give something to the poor. Why would they think that he went to give something to the poor? Obviously, Jesus regularly gave to the poor. Could this be the reason Judas was able to steal without the other disciples knowing? Could it be that Jesus would say to Judas, "Go give $500 to the poor widow we met yesterday." Imagine Judas graciously going to the widow's tent and saying to her, "Jesus sent me to give you $300"?

Jesus had enough money in the treasury to hire eighty-two workers, to allow Judas to steal on a regular basis without the other disciples knowing, and to regularly give to the poor. What an abundance Jesus must have had in His treasury.

What Jesus would have given indicates that He was not poor. On one particularly noteworthy day in the life of Jesus, He had been teaching His disciples along with some others who had followed Him. Being late in the day, they had become hungry, "Therefore Jesus, lifting up His eyes and seeing that a large crowd was coming to Him, said to Philip, 'Where are we to buy bread, so that these may eat?'" (John

6:5). Notice that Jesus did not ask, "What are we are going to buy the bread with?" but rather, "Where are we going to buy it?" Obviously, He had enough money to buy the bread to feed them. Apparently Philip believed that He did. "Phillip answered Him, "Two hundred denarii worth of bread is not sufficient for them, for everyone to receive a little'" (verse 7). Why would Phillip mention 200 denarii? Did he just pull that number out of thin air? Not likely. Phillip must have had that much money himself, left over from what Jesus had given to him, or he had some reason to believe that there was at least that much money in Jesus' treasury.

How Jesus distinguished Himself from the poor indicates that He was not poor. He did it in a way that was not disparaging, but encouraging. To Judas who raised this question, "Why was this perfume not sold for three hundred denarii and given to poor people?" (John 12:5), Jesus gave this answer: "For you always have the poor with you, but you do not always have Me" (verse 8). Judas had raised the question "not because he was concerned about the poor, but because he was a thief" (verse 6).

Notice that Jesus said, "You will have the poor," not "You should be poor." Jesus was not saying that we should be poor so that the poor could have company. Many people are poor because they do not know how to manage money and are not interested in learning how. If we do not learn how to manage our money, whatever we have will likely get away from us.

Jesus was really saying, "You will always have the poor with you, but you will not always have Me." That is a powerful way of saying, "I'm not poor! I am not in that category."

How would we react if someone poured $1,000,000 worth of cologne over our feet? We probably would be thinking a little bit like Judas thought. "Why wasn't this sold and used to pay off my bills and build me a house?" Those who are unaccustomed to the finer things of life tend to become apologetic when the finer things of life are bestowed upon them. Jesus was not at all disturbed by this lavish behavior. His thinking and behavior are not at all the thinking and behavior of a poor person. His welcome response paralleled the lifestyles of the rich and famous.

We should always read Scripture carefully. Otherwise, we may miss significant details that God wants to use to revolutionize our spiritual paradigm. Our preconceived mind may cause us to fail to see that Jesus wore tailor-made clothing. "Then the soldiers, when they had crucified Jesus, took His outer garments and made four parts, a part to every soldier and also the tunic; now the tunic was seamless, woven in one piece" (John 19:23). Today we all wear clothes that have been sewn. Jesus wore tailor-made clothes. His garments did not have a seam. Those who crucified Him gambled for His garments. Who gambles for the rags of a poor person? Jesus was not poor.

What Jesus received at birth indicates that He was not poor.

> Now after Jesus was born in Bethlehem of Judea
> in the days of Herod the king, magi from the east
> arrived in Jerusalem, saying, "Where is He who
> has been born King of the Jews? For we saw His
> star in the east and have come to worship
> Him"...When they saw the star, they rejoiced
> exceedingly with great joy. After coming into the
> house they saw the Child with Mary His mother;
> and they fell to the ground and worshiped Him.
> Then, opening their treasures, they presented to
> Him gifts of gold, frankincense, and myrrh.
> (Matthew 2:1-2, 10-11).

The magi did not bring gifts for a beggar; they brought gifts for a king. There is a different type of gift one gives to a king. When Jesus was born, He received a king's portion of precious items: gold, frankincense, and myrrh. I do not know how much a king's portion was, but we can refer to an earlier occasion when a king received his portion of gold from his admirer.

> Now when the queen of Sheba heard of the fame
> of Solomon, she came to Jerusalem to test
> Solomon with difficult questions. She had a very
> large retinue, with camels carrying spices and a
> large amount of gold and precious stones; and

when she came to Solomon, she spoke with him about all that was on her heart...Then she gave the king one hundred and twenty talents of gold and a very great amount of spices and precious stones; there had never been spice like that which the queen of Sheba gave to King Solomon (2 Chronicles 9:1, 9).

A talent of gold was equivalent to 100 pounds, and worth approximately $5,760,000. That gives us an idea of what a king's portion is.

Some have drawn the wrong conclusion that Jesus' parents were poor just because He was born in a manger. However, a careful reading of the text reveals the reason; there was no vacancy in the inn. "And she gave birth to her firstborn son; and she wrapped Him in cloths, and laid Him in a manger, because there was no room for them in the inn" (Luke 2:7). When Joseph and Mary arrived in Bethlehem, they found many other people who had also arrived to register for the census. For whatever reason, the rooms were filled. The text does not say that Jesus was born in a manger because His parents were poor, but rather that there was no room in the inn. Even today, those who start a journey without making hotel reservations may find themselves in a distant city expecting a place to stay, but finding none. Even with the financial means, if there is no vacancy, they must embrace the consequences.

We need to understand the financial strength of Jesus because it will help us in our situations. Would Jesus have been able to minister so compassionately if He had been worrying about finances? Would He have been able to teach His disciples to give freely if they had been in poverty? Not likely. Knowing that Jesus was a man of means helps us not to feel guilty during our healthy pursuit of economic resources.

WHEN JESUS WAS POOR

Through Moses, God promised prosperity to those who will obey His will. "So keep the words of this covenant to do them, that you may prosper in all that you do" (Deuteronomy 29:9). To Joshua, again God promised prosperity and success to those who obey His will. "Only be strong and very courageous; be careful to do according to all the law which Moses My servant commanded you; do not turn from it to the right or to the left, so that you may have success wherever you go" (Joshua 1:7). To King David, God said:

> "Only the Lord give you discretion and understanding, and give you charge over Israel, so that you may keep the law of the Lord your God. Then you will prosper, if you are careful to observe the statutes and the ordinances which the Lord commanded Moses concerning Israel. Be strong and courageous, do not fear nor be dismayed" (1 Chronicles 22:12-13).

Why would the Lord give understanding? Does He give understanding just for argument's sake? Absolutely not. The Lord gives understanding to His people so that they can do according to His understanding. His understanding exceeds human understanding. When we surrender to His understanding we use a superior wisdom. Certainly, we need the superior wisdom operating within our economic entities.

God promised prosperity to those who would walk in His will. The apostle Peter reminds us how perfectly Jesus walked in the will of the Father:

> For you have been called for this purpose, since Christ also suffered for you, leaving you an example for you to follow in His steps, who committed no sin, nor was any deceit found in His mouth; and while being reviled, He did not revile in return; while suffering, He uttered no threats, but kept entrusting Himself to Him who judges righteously (1 Peter 2:21-23).

Since Jesus walked in the will of God, what should we have expected the Father to do? At least we should expect God to keep His promise. He promised Jesus blessings in everything that He did. It would have been wrong for God not to have blessed Him because that is what He promised to do. God cannot lie! If anyone should have received the prosperity of God, it should have been Jesus.

So why does the prosperity of Jesus surprise people? I do not know where the church gets the poverty mindset that Jesus was a beggar walking around with absolutely nothing. It did not come from the Scriptures. As a matter of fact, we should expect Jesus to have been abundantly prosperous in everything that He put in His head and His hand to do.

When did Jesus become poor? Jesus became poor on the cross.

> Now when Jesus saw a crowd around Him, He gave orders to depart to the other side of the sea. Then a scribe came and said to Him, "Teacher, I will follow You wherever You go." Jesus said to him, "The foxes have holes and the birds of the air have nests, but the Son of Man has nowhere to lay His head" (Matthew 8:18-20).

Now what does that mean? I believe that Jesus was talking about where He would lay His head in death. Indeed, He did not have a burial ground. He had nowhere to lay his head in death; therefore they buried him in Joseph's new tomb. Jesus became poor on the cross and remained poor while He was in the grave. Jesus relinquished everything He had for the three days that He was in the grave.

Why did Jesus become poor? Jesus became poor in the sense that He left all His heavenly riches in order to come to earth to bless us.

Have this attitude in yourselves which was also in Christ Jesus, who, although He existed in the form of God, did not regard equality with God a thing to be grasped, but emptied Himself, taking the form of a bond-servant, and being made in the likeness of men. Being found in appearance as a man, He humbled Himself by becoming obedient to the point of death, even death on a cross (Philippians 2:5-8).

Where would we be if Jesus had not given up His heavenly riches? We would be of all men most miserable. Before and after the cross, Jesus had the capacity to obtain everything that He wanted and to do everything that He needed. Whatever Jesus did have was by choice. There was not one time when Jesus wanted something and did not have the things that He needed in order to do it. It does not get any better than that. Jesus was a wealthy carpenter. He could have built or bought a house if He wanted one. There really is no indication that Jesus did not have a house.

If Jesus had been financially poor, how would that help us financially and spiritually? It would not, because we are helped only by what He gave us. An example of poverty does not help us. If it is God's will to be poor, then we should get in poverty, stay in poverty, and do everything we can to remain in poverty for all of life. If it is God's will to be poor, then it is sinful not to be poor.

Therefore, since we have a great high priest who has passed through the heavens, Jesus the Son of God, let us hold fast our confession. For we do not have a high priest who cannot sympathize with our weaknesses, but One who has been tempted in all things as we are, yet without sin. Therefore let us draw near with confidence to the throne of grace, so that we may receive mercy and find grace to help in time of need (Hebrews 4:14-16).

The Hebrew writer is saying we come to God through the cross, but we move from the cross to the throne. The cross is about sacrifice, but the throne is about living in the abundances of God! God wants us to draw near to the throne. The throne is not where we go to give; it is where we go to receive and to worship. God has made a promise that at the throne of grace we may receive mercy and find help in a time of need. The throne radiates the concept of wisdom. That is why Isaiah said, "I saw the Lord seated on a throne, high and exalted, and the train of his robe filled the temple" (Isaiah 6:1). When we come to the throne of God, it is time for joyous celebration. That is why worship is always pictured at the throne, not at the cross. Worship is not about dying; it is about living! He calls us from the cross to the throne. They are two different lifestyles. If we live at the cross, we will still get to heaven. Yes, we will miss hell in the afterlife, but we will likely live in misery while on earth.

THOUGHT PROVOKERS

1. How difficult will it be to reverse the almost universal belief that Jesus was poverty stricken? How would Jesus being financially poor help others who are poor?

2. How does the knowledge of Jesus being rich impact your attitude toward wealth?

3. What do you think happened to the wealth that Jesus received at birth?

Chapter 4

GOD'S ECONOMIC SYSTEM

G od is a systematic God, and He functions according to a system. God designed the universe as a system. A system consists of patterns, principles, and procedures—established ways of doing things. He created the universe as a system, and He created within this system patterns, principles, and procedures—so we actually have systems within a system.

God created the heavens as a system; within the heavens, He created the stars, the sun, and the moon—systems within a system! God designed the human being as a system; each person is a spirit, possessing a soul, and living in a body. The human body is a system of systems: the cardiovascular system, the circulatory system, the nervous system, and a number of other systems. We are a system that contains a number of other systems.

In addition to designing the visible material universe as a system, God also designed an invisible, immaterial universe. There is more to life than what meets the eye. When we look at a person, there is more to that person than just what we see. Similarly, there is more to the universe than just what we see. God created an invisible immaterial universe within the visible, material universe. At the same time, He designed invisible patterns, principles, and procedures; within patterns, principles, and procedures; within patterns, principles, and procedures; within patterns, principles, and procedures, and so on. God has placed invisible principles within the universe to guide and guard the visible universe.

God's thoughts are superior to all human thoughts. "'For My thoughts are not your thoughts, nor are your ways My ways,' declares the Lord. 'For as the heavens are higher than the earth, so are My ways higher than your ways and My thoughts than your thoughts'" (Isaiah 55:8-9). God is a thinker. If we want to be like God, we must learn to think like He thinks. Our best thinking comes when we train ourselves to think like God. Whenever we abandon God's thinking, we are taking a step downward. Parents say to their children, "I understand what you are saying. I've been through this. I know what you are thinking. I know a little better than you. My thoughts are a little better than yours." Their children, however, don't believe them. How could their parents possibly understand what they're thinking or going through? Similarly, we don't believe that God thinks better than we do, or that His thoughts are higher than our thoughts. We say, "Yeah, but...yeah, but..."

Now, God has some thoughts and He has some ways, as we saw in Isaiah 55:8. He says, "As the rain and the snow come down from heaven, and do not return there without watering the earth and making it bear and sprout, and furnishing seed to the sower and bread to the eater" (Isaiah 55:10). Where does the rain come from? Heaven. Where does the snow come from? Heaven. We shouldn't ever again complain about rain and snow! If we ever again wonder why there is so much rain or so much snow, we should reread these verses. Rain and snow come for a purpose: to water the earth so that it will grow and we will have something to eat. If it stops raining, in a little while all of us will be on a forced fast.

If the water comes down from heaven, my question is, "How does it get there?" Amos 5:8 gives us the answer: "He who made the Pleiades and Orion and changes deep darkness into morning, who also darkens day into night, who calls for the waters of the sea and pours them out on the surface of the earth, the Lord is His name." God Himself calls the waters of the sea and then pours them out on the earth. These verses have just described evaporation and condensation. That's an invisible principle that guides and guards the material universe. When God created the universe, He placed therein a pattern, a principle, and a procedure for watering the earth—condensation and evaporation.

Just as God has scientific systems for running the universe, He has an economic system. It consists of patterns, principles, and procedures that govern our economic experiences. It may surprise us to know that the devil has also designed an economic system. His economic system also consists of patterns, principles, and procedures. Guess what? Just like God works through the design of His system, the devil works through the design of his system. God has an economic system, and the devil has an economic system. God's system has patterns, principles, and procedures; the devil's system has patterns, principles, and procedures. Both economic systems—whether God's system or the devil's system—were designed to do two things: to guide and to guard in the acquiring and managing of economic resources. The end results of following these two systems, however, could not be more different, as we will see.

We must ask ourselves, "Whose system am I following?" Likely, many of us are not following God's system. We came into the world introduced to the devils' system. Quickly, we embraced the devil's system and thought that is the way it's supposed to be.

Remember Archie Bunker and his wife, Edith? When Archie came home from work, Edith took his coat, ran to fetch him a beer, and settled him into his easy chair. If we grew up in a household and our momma just ran and got every thing for our father, we may have thought that was the way it was supposed to be. Why? We were born into that system. No doubt most of us came up in an environment where our family used the devil's economic system. It was out of alignment and caused much pain—yet we kept following it.

God says, "Do what is right and I will give you more than you need."

How does God's economic system work? God says, "Do what is right and I will give you more than you need." He said that at the beginning of creation (see Genesis 1:26-29) and He renewed His promise to Abram (see Genesis 12:1-4). That may seem amazing to us. "Do what's right and I'll give you more than you need." What an awesome God we serve!

How does the devil's system work? The devil says, "Do not wait until God gives you something; take what you want." In fact, the devil says, "Take it even before you need it." Had Adam and Eve eaten all the fruit in the garden? They weren't hungry. They already had plenty of food to eat, but they decided to take what God had placed off limits. If we are under the devil's system, we cannot expect the blessings of God. We can expect only the rewards that the devil produces.

The financial system we choose affects every aspect of our lives. We must remove the notion far from our minds that we can operate in the wrong system and yet remain spiritual. While we operate in the wrong system, all of life is misaligned. Many people who are in the wrong system get mad at God because they cannot pray themselves out of it. If we are on the wrong bus, we cannot pray ourselves to the right destination. We must get off that bus and get on the right bus. We must get out of the devil's economic system and get into God's economic system. Satan's economic system always fails! If we are in satan's economic system, we are doomed to fail. If we play the money game according to the devil's rules, we will always lose. Some keep losing because they keep playing according to the devil's system.

Moses recognized that if he would get out of God's faith system and into the devil's system, gain would be short lived.

> By faith Moses, when he was born, was hidden
> for three months by his parents, because they saw
> he was a beautiful child; and they were not afraid
> of the king's edict. By faith Moses, when he had
> grown up, refused to be called the son of
> Pharaoh's daughter, choosing rather to endure ill-

treatment with the people of God than to enjoy the passing pleasures of sin (Hebrews 11:23-25).

God's economic system always succeeds. When we play according to God's rule, we always succeed. Moses considered the Christ whom He looked forward to far greater riches than the treasures of Egypt (see Hebrews 11:26-27). Therefore, he endured not fearing the wrath of the king. He knew that God's reward was well worth the painful effort. Moses took his eyes off the visible and focused on the invisible, recognizing that the invisible principles, patterns, and procedures would ultimately bring about much more than the visible, material things that Egypt had to offer.

God wants us to learn and honor His system. When we do honor God's economic system, we can live without fear. If we are living with financial fear, it may indicate that we have failed to honor God's economic system.

When we live within God's system, we've got something to look forward to. Moses was looking forward to great eternal joys. If we are not in God's system, where we are living now is as good as it gets. We can't look forward to heaven, and hell is worse than this. Therefore, please accept this invitation into God's system. Through faith, repentance, and baptism, we enter into His Kingdom. Therein we learn God's economic system and participate in the responsibilities and privileges.

God is creative in nature, and He also is administrative in nature. Everything that God has created includes guidelines to tell us how it ought to work. When General Motors makes a new car, they put together an owner's manual for the owner. They put together a repair manual to tell the repair person how this machine is best supposed to function. God's Word tells us how all His systems work to guide and guard us—including His economic system. He even contrasts both systems—His and the devil's—to show us how they work and what we can expect from each. Certainly, we need to know the difference.

God's economic system, patterns, principles, and procedures contribute to our character development, while the devil's economic system contributes to our character destruction. When we have done it God's way, our character is improved, but when we have done it satan's way, our character is compromised. Thievery, thuggery, and false balances are not God's way (see Proverbs 20:10). The devil offered Jesus some things (see Luke chapter 4), but the price tag was too high. Jesus would have to fall down and worship. The devil makes the same empty offer to us, with the same high price. Even now, he says, "I will give you all this. I will give you the houses. I will give you the cars. I will give you the jewelry. I will give you clothes. I will give you the vacations. I will give you the fame and stardom. I will give you all these things—just fall down and worship me."

People accumulate merchandise through the devil's system, yet they ask God through prayer to protect it. God's economic system promotes unselfishness. Satan's system promotes selfishness. Notice how many times the rich man referred to "I," "me," or "mine" in Luke 12:17-19. Notice how God's system breeds an altruistic spirit while the devil's system breeds selfishness. Notice how the story started (see verse 13). A man came to Jesus and said, "Tell my brother to give me one of Daddy's two cars! Tell my brother to give me half the stuff that was in Grandmomma's trunk! Tell my sister to give me half of Daddy's bank account!"

And Jesus said, "Who made Me an arbiter over you?" Two brothers were fighting; one had some things, but he got them because he was selfish. The other brother simply wanted some stuff. Both were selfish. Selfishness has ripped families right down the middle, destroying them because of greed. Selfishness and greed have caused more heartache after loved ones have died than the deaths themselves. Siblings fight over stuff, over money, over property. It is not worth it to tear apart a family. God's system doesn't have people selfishly falling out over stuff. I once spent the night in the home of a man who was later killed by his twin brother. Rumor was that his brother killed him because of a money dispute. Not only did his brother kill him, but he also killed his brother's wife, his sister, and his own mother—all because of "stuff." Satan's system deceives us into being selfish.

The rich man was a fool. He was a fool not because he was wealthy. He was a fool because he was not wealthy toward God. Satan's economic system breeds selfishness, which causes us to worry. Jesus told the story about worrying right after He finished talking about covetousness. We worry about whether something is going to happen to the stuff that we obtained through satan's system in the first place. If God gave it to us, we would have the attitude, "He gave it to me once. He'll give it to me again." That's why Job didn't worry. He said, "I came into this world with nothing. God gave me what I've got. If He wants me to have some more, He'll give it to me. If He takes this, He'll give me some more." Therefore, we should honor God and His economic system.

THOUGHT PROVOKERS

1. Do you find it difficult to trust God and His economic system to sustain you? Why or why not?

2. Contrast the components of God's economic system with satan's economic system? How are they similar? How are they different?

3. How can you encourage others to subscribe to God's economic system?

Chapter 5

BLESSINGS OF STEWARDSHIP

A steward is a temporary custodian over the resources of another. Stewards use their God-given abilities to manage their God-given resources to accomplish their God-intended results (see 1 Corinthians 4:1-7, Colossians 1:25, 1 Peter 4:10). For forty years, King David ruled over all of Israel, yet he recognized that he was just a steward:

> So David blessed the Lord in the sight of all the assembly; and David said, "Blessed are You, O Lord God of Israel our father, forever and ever. Yours, O Lord, is the greatness and the power and the glory and the victory and the majesty, indeed everything that is in the heavens and the earth; Yours is the dominion, O Lord, and You exalt

Yourself as head over all. Both riches and honor come from You, and You rule over all, and in Your hand is power and might; and it lies in Your hand to make great and to strengthen everyone… But who am I and who are my people that we should be able to offer as generously as this? For all things come from You, and from Your hand we have given You. For we are sojourners before You, and tenants, as all our fathers were; our days on the earth are like a shadow, and there is no hope. O Lord our God, all this abundance that we have provided to build You a house for Your holy name, it is from Your hand, and all is Yours" (1 Chronicles 29:10-12, 14-16).

We too are just stewards, and we must work to become good stewards. God is the source of all our blessings. He possesses the power to give us all that we need (see above verses and 1 Corinthians 4:7). God is also the source of all His own blessings. He possesses the passion to give to Himself all that He needs (see above verses and 2 Corinthians 9:6, 8-15). Those who give always have something to give.

A father took his son to McDonald's and bought him some fries. After a few moments, the father reached over to get two fries, but the son quickly snatched them back and said, "No!" The father persisted, but the son emphatically said, "No!" The father then thought, (1) "Doesn't my son know that I am the reason he has fries?" (2) "That I could take his fries?" (3) "That I could buy myself fries?" (4) "That I could buy enough fries to bury him under?" (5) "That I really do not like fries?" (6) "That I really do not need fries?" (7) "That all I need is my son's willingness to share with me what I have shared with him?"

We are accountable to God for what He has blessed us with, for indeed He is the source of all our blessings. God gives to us so that we can give to Him and to His people. He requires only what He has previously given to us.

Hurriedly but humbly, a moral, mannered rich man approached Jesus. This man graciously greeted the Master and asked, "What shall I do to inherit eternal life?" (Mark 10:17). Jesus questioned the rich man's motive for his greeting and directed his attention to the commandments. This rich man claimed to have kept all the commandments from his youth up. Jesus then gave the rich man the stewardship test—and he failed miserably. Stewards use their God-given abilities to manage their God-given resources to accomplish God-intended results. Good stewards realize that they are just temporary custodial managers over the resources of another. The rich young man failed to realize this, and in failing to become a good steward, he remained spiritually unfulfilled.

The story of the good Samaritan in Luke 10:30-37 can teach us a good deal about various attitudes toward stewardship. The first attitude is, "What is yours is mine, and I am going to get it" (see verse 30). The robber exhibited this attitude. Excessive taxation revolves upon this principle (see Romans 13:6), as does the lottery (see Ephesians 4:28).

What is gambling? Gambling is risking the loss of resources in an artificial, created, and unnecessary scheme in an attempt to obtain what belongs to another, without rendering a constructive product (service or merchandise of equivalent value) in return. Some will say that all of life is a gamble for it involves a risk. That may be true, but the lottery is the form of gambling wherein the risk is (1) artificial, (2) created, (3) unnecessary, and (4) through that risk one obtains what belongs to another while not providing a constructive product or value in return.

What is the motivation for gambling? Some will say they gamble to contribute to worthy causes. Let me suggest that we visit the bet-placing station and ask the patrons to contribute to the "worthy cause." Will they? No! Obviously they do not gamble because they wish to contribute to the cause. Let me suggest that we visit the bet-placing station and ask the patrons to contribute to our personal bank accounts. Will they? No! Obviously they do not gamble because they wish for us to have their funds.

Where does the money come from that the winners receive? It comes from the money that previously belonged to the losers. What happens when someone wins the lottery? He or she receives the losers' money; the losers did not want the winner to have that money, yet the winner receives that money without giving the losers any constructive product or value in return. Think about that! Winners receive losers' money, and return no constructive product or value. Losers did not want winners to have their money.

Would this apply anywhere else in society? Is there any place that we obtain another's resources without giving them a constructive product or value in return? Anywhere else in society, we would call that cheating, stealing, or robbery (see Ephesians 4:28).

If we gamble with someone, we treat them in a manner in which we do not want them to treat us, for we do not want them to have our money (see Matthew 7:12). Therefore, the lottery is inconsistent with Christianity. Gambling promotes the spirit of obtaining something for nothing (see 2 Thessalonians 3:6-10). Therefore, the lottery is inconsistent with Christianity.

Remove the element of potential gain and then let folk participate in the scheme. How many would still participate in the gambling scheme without the potential for gain? Few to none would participate. Personal greed is the spirit that motivates gambling. Therefore, the lottery is inconsistent with Christianity.

If the gambling venture gives away $2,000,000, those who gambled could have pooled their resources, produced a company, and provided jobs; even if they lost $2,000,000, they would have still provided a much better service to society. Gambling, whether through the lottery or other means, is an extremely poor use of resources. Gambling does not promote good stewardship.

What about the stock market? The stock market differs from the lottery because investors who purchase stock are lending their money to the company that sells the stock. If the company makes a profit, it returns a portion of the profits to the stockholders, or the value of stockholders' ownership increases, all things being equal.

The state cannot legislate virtue, but it should refuse to sanction vice. I am not encouraging Christians to picket establishments that promote gambling (such as a grocery store that sells lottery tickets), but I am suggesting that Christians should refuse to participate in the gambling schemes.

The second attitude toward stewardship that we see in the story of the good Samaritan is, "What is mine is mine, and I am going to keep it" (see Luke 10:31-32). The priest and Levite exhibited this attitude. Admit it: We sort of like this attitude. These people took nothing that did not belong to them and they hurt no one. What is wrong with that? They were like those who ate their picnic in the park. When finished, they removed their tablecloth, threw away the trash, and didn't leave any extra food lying around—but they forgot that someone had planted the trees for shade and built the table for comfort. Therefore, they never thought to replenish for the next generation. No doubt the priest and the Levite felt they were too busy to take the time to stop and help the hurting man. No doubt they felt they were too poor. Whatever their attitude was that caused them to keep walking, it was wrong.

The third attitude we see in this parable is, "What is mine is yours, and I am going to give it." The Samaritan exhibited this attitude (see verses 33-37). He gave his time and he gave his money. He had the right attitude about being a steward over what had been given to him.

There were similarities in all these people, in spite of their different reactions. They all saw the same need. They all had something to do and somewhere else to go. They all could have offered excuses: The priest and the Levite may have offered a theological excuse. After all, if they had touched a dead body, they would be rendered unclean. "The one who touches the corpse of any person shall be unclean for seven days" (Numbers 19:11). If he became unclean, he could not perform his priestly duties. The Samaritan could have offered a social excuse. After all, the Jews did not have any social dealing with the Samaritans (see John 4:9).

There were also differences in their reactions. The robber thought, "What is yours is mine, and I am going to get it." The priest and Levite thought, "What is mine is mine, and I am going to keep it." The good Samaritan knew that God gives tomorrow based on what we give today (see Matthew 25:23).

We must separate ourselves from all that prevents our spiritual fulfillment.

Refusing to become a good steward will leave us spiritually unfulfilled. How can we become good stewards? We must separate ourselves from all that prevents our spiritual fulfillment. Jesus ordered the rich young man to invest his resources in the kingdom work of God. "Go and sell all you possess and give to the poor, and you will have treasure in heaven; and come, follow Me" (Mark 10:21). If this man had invested his resources in the kingdom work of God, he would have received a great earthly reward (see Mark 10:28-30, Matthew 25:14-29).

What is holding back our spiritual fulfillment? Is our third job keeping us from Bible study, worship, fellowship, prayer, and spiritual meditation? Why do we have a third job? We need it to pay for our fourth TV. Why do we need a fourth TV? We need it to put in our fifth bedroom so that our sixth cousin will have something to watch every seventh month when he comes to visit.

If we want to be spiritually fulfilled, we must not only separate ourselves from all that prevents it, but we must also saturate ourselves with all that promotes our spiritual fulfillment. Jesus ordered the rich young man to invest himself in the kingdom work of God. "Come, follow Me" (Mark 10:21). If this man had invested himself in the kingdom work of God, he would have received a great eternal reward (see Mark 10:28-30, Matthew 25:31-46). Refusing to become a good steward leaves us spiritually unfulfilled. This man jeopardized his earthly and eternal spiritual fulfillment (see Mark 10:21).

The choice of becoming a good steward or a bad one is up to us—and so are the blessings or consequences that will follow.

THOUGHT PROVOKERS

1. What do you have that prevents your spiritual fulfillment?

2. How do you have what you have that prevents your spiritual fulfillment? What are you so attached to that your attachment hinders your spiritual fulfillment? What possessions do you have (or what possessions have you) that the very thought of sharing them or separating from them causes you anxiety?

3. What promotes your spiritual fulfillment?

Chapter 6

EXERCISE 1: RECOGNIZE THAT GOD OWNS IT ALL

In the next seven chapters, we will look at seven exercises that will help us to build economic strength by taking control of our finances. Remember, these are not "seven simple steps" to help us get out of debt or become wealthy overnight. They are not a quick fix-all to wipe out our credit-card debt and give us more money to spend unwisely. These are exercises based on the tried and true principles that God has set out for us in His Word. When we apply them diligently and with commitment, they will help us to move from financial stress to financial stability to financial strength.

The first exercise is to recognize that God owns it all. We may think we know this in our heads, but we do not always act as if we do. God is the creator. He is the creator of everything, including all the economic resources. Genesis 1:1 says, "In the beginning God created the heavens and the earth." That is a very clear summary of what He created: everything in heaven and everything on earth. God Himself is the creator of our time and energy. He is the creator of our intelligence and our opportunities. God enables us to obtain our resources and achieve our economic standing. Nothing we have or have achieved originated with us. "For who regards you as superior? What do you have that you did not receive? And if you did receive it, why do you boast as if you had not received it?" (1 Corinthians 4:7).

Our resources come from Him. "For the earth is the Lord's and all it contains" (1 Corinthians 10:26). Our time comes from Him. In fact, He is the owner of our time. It was He who decided that there would be twenty-four hours in a day, seven days in a week, and 365 days in a year. Our energy comes from Him. He is the creator of our energy. Our strength did not originate with our assimilation of Wheaties. If God had not put energy potential into the food stuff from which Wheaties come, we would remain impotent even after eating our fill. After eating, God activates our bodies so that they will absorb nutrition and assimilate it into energy.

Our intelligence comes from Him. He is the creator of our intelligence. We did not simply inherit our intelligence from our ancestors. In the beginning of our human ancestry, God gave wisdom to Adam. Adam was smart. He named everything and remembered the names thereafter. Only a highly intelligent being could do this. Adam's intelligence, like ours, came from God.

God created this universe and has established ownership of all the resources. It all belongs to Him. He owns it all, including all the money. "The earth is the Lord's, and all it contains, the world, and those who dwell in it" (Psalm 24:1). Therefore, all that any person has really belongs to God.

God declared that godly disciples were complete without economic resources. In the beginning, human beings came into the world bringing no economic resources. "For we have brought nothing into the world" (1 Timothy 6:7a). In the end, they left this world taking no economic resources. "So we cannot take anything out of it either" (1 Timothy 6:7b).

A wealthy man said to his wife, "Honey, I am going to take my money with me when I die." When he became deathly ill, he decided to put all his money in the attic. Some time thereafter, he died. His wife went into the attic and saw that all the money remained there. She said, "I knew that he should have put it in the basement." Of course, wherever he put it would not have mattered. We cannot take our money with us when we die.

RECOGNIZE THAT GOD IS THE ADMINISTRATOR

God is the creator and the owner—the creative owner—of everything, and we need to honor Him as such. Because God is the creative owner, He qualifies to be the administrative owner. He reserves the right to tell us what to do with what we have. If we waste a resource that He has given to us—time, energy, or intelligence—we waste a resource from God.

Since God is the creator of all our economic resources (see Genesis 1:1, Acts 17:24), and since He is the creator of time, energy, and intelligence (see 1 Corinthians 4:7), then He is also owner (see 1 Corinthians 10:26, Psalm 24:1). Therefore, we need to honor God as our creative owner. Since God is creator of all our economic resources and the owner of them, He is also the administrator of them (see Genesis 1:6, 9, 11, 26-30, Acts 17:24-31). He is the administrator of our time, energy, and intelligence (see Exodus 19:5). Since He is administrator, He can tell us how to view our economic standing and how to use our economic resources (see 1 Timothy 6:17-10). Therefore, we need to honor God as our administrative owner.

RECOGNIZE THAT GOD IS THE CENTERPIECE OF OUR ECONOMIC SUFFICIENCY

God established and communicated His standard for determining economic sufficiency. "If we have food and covering, with these we shall be *content*" (1 Timothy 6:8). Within this context, the word *content* means "to have a feeling of self sufficiency or self satisfaction." The original Greek word that was translated as *content* was used in two other instances in the New Testament: "Some soldiers were questioning him [John the Baptist], saying, 'And what about us, what shall we do?' And he said to them, 'Do not take money from anyone by force, or accuse anyone falsely, and be *content* with your wages" (Luke 3:14 emphasis added). The other is "Make sure that your character is free from the love of money, being *content* with what you have; for He Himself has said, 'I will never desert you, nor will I ever forsake you'" (Hebrews 13:5 emphasis added).

God established the basis upon which we should be content and satisfied. We should accept God's standard for determining our economic sufficiency. What is God's standard? In the beginning, God provided internal nourishments for the body. He gave the food of the garden to Adam and Eve. God provided all the food necessary to nourish them (see Genesis 1:29, 2:15).

Also, God provided an environmental enclosure for the body. He did not leave Adam on the outside. He placed him on the inside of something. Initially, He placed Adam within the garden. "The Lord God planted a garden toward the east, in Eden; and there He placed the man whom He had formed" (Genesis 2:8). After they had eaten from the forbidden tree,

God provided for them another environmental enclosure. "The Lord God made garments of skin for Adam and his wife, and clothed them" (Genesis 3:21).

That is why God would later remind His people that when they had internal nourishments (food) and external coverings they should be content. If food and covering are what we need to be content, then everything above food and covering is a luxury! Yes, our cell phone, cablevision, and even the television set itself are all luxuries. God never said we could not have luxuries; we just need to admit to ourselves when we are reveling in luxuries.

He sustains us because of His promise, not because of our performance.

RECOGNIZE THAT GOD IS THE CENTERPIECE OF OUR ECONOMIC STABILITY

We must recognize that God is the center of our economic stability. He sustains us because of His promise, not because of our performance. No matter how wealthy or comfortable we become, we are sustained due to His promise, not our performance. In fact, it is God who decided to favor us in the first place (see Deuteronomy 8:14-15)—and He favors us in spite of where we are and the circumstances we encounter. He warns us not to think that our success is due only to our own power and strength (see Deuteronomy 8:16-17).

God is the center of our economic stability—and He has given us the power to make wealth. He sustains us and gives us power, intelligence, and opportunities to accumulate the results of our economic stability, yet some people claim the credit, saying, "I just selected the right stocks to invest in." Why does God give us the power to make wealth? He does so because it is the way He confirms His covenant with us: "But you shall remember the Lord your God, for it is He who is giving you power to make wealth, that He may confirm His covenant which He swore to your fathers, as it is this day" (Deuteronomy 8:18). Now, isn't that just awesome? God made a promise to Abram (Abraham). He promised to bless Abram and those who would bless Abram. Therefore, God had to make good on His promise. Therefore, He sustains us not because of our performance, but because of His promise.

When we recognize that God is the center of our economic sufficiency and stability, the enjoyment of His blessings should provoke our thankfulness. The next time an arrogant person asks, "Why should I worship God?" we should tell him how well things are going for us. Worshiping God is one way to say, "Thank You." We should come together and sing praises to

God as a resounding thanks for the things that God has already done. Unfortunately, many do not come and worship until they want another favor from God. In view of the bread of heaven, we should give thanks for the food on the table. In view of the robe of righteousness, we should give thanks for the clothes on our back. In view of our eternal home in heaven, we should give thanks for the house on the block.

When we recognize that God is the center of our economic stability, then we look at promotions, raises, and bonuses differently. We realize they have elevated our economic perspective, and we give God thanks. Our first thought is not, "What else can I buy at the mall?" but rather, "How can I express thanks?"

Our tendency, however, is to forget. Moses explained in Deuteronomy 8:11-14 that the people's problem was forgetfulness. They forgot that God was the centerpiece of their economic sufficiency and stability—and because they forgot, they pushed God to the side. God reminded His people to remember Him: "Beware lest you forget the Lord your God by not keeping His commandments and His ordinances and His statutes which I am commanding you today" (Deuteronomy 8:11). What is God doing? First, God equated forgetfulness with disobedience, and remembrance with obedience. Second, He reminded them to remember so that they could obey. Failure to keep the commandment indicated that they had forgotten. Keeping the command indicated that they remembered. God also reminded them of the stiff penalty for forgetting:

> "It shall come about if you ever forget the Lord your God and go after other gods and serve them and worship them, I testify against you today that you will surely perish. Like the nations that the Lord makes to perish before you, so you shall perish; because you would not listen to the voice of the Lord your God" (Deuteronomy 8:19-20).

He equated forgetfulness with disobedience because one cannot do what one fails to remember to do. When we were little, our parents would send us to the store with the instructions, "Buy bread—and bread only. Do not spend any money on candy." Instead of buying bread, we bought a Baby Ruth bar. Why? We forgot. Forgetfulness is equated with disobedience, because we cannot do the commandments of God if we forget the commandments of God. Therefore, He reminded His people to remember Him. Not only did He remind them not to forget Him, but He also assigned an amnesia penalty. He promised destruction to those who forgot and failed to keep the commandments. Those who forgot no longer kept His commandments. Those who no longer kept His commandments obviously had forgotten.

We must remember so that we can behave as if God, not our wise ability to select particular stocks, is the centerpiece of our economic strength. The further we get from our harsh realities, the less God-conscious we become. What do people automatically do when something harsh happens to them? They cry out, "Oh God!" Suddenly, they remember Him. What do people automatically do when something wonderful happens? They are not likely to think about God—not likely at all.

We can become so wealthy that we forget who is the center of our economic sufficiency and stability. We can become so prosperous that we forget. God warns us that our heart will become proud and we will forget the Lord our God who brought us out of the land of Egypt, and out of the land of slavery (see Deuteronomy 8:14). It happens on an individual basis. When we couldn't afford a vacation, we'd come to church every Sunday. Now that we can afford a vacation, we are vacating on Sunday, missing worship. Now, we are so prosperous that we have just vacated God right out of the picture! The further we get from our harsh realities, the less God-conscious we become. We forget that God owns it all.

It happens on a family basis, too. Disaster strikes, poverty sets in, and the family gets together to pray, but when everybody gets a job and is doing extra well, suddenly there is no time for Bible study, no time for prayer, and no time for family devotion. The more prosperous we become and the further we get from our harsh realities, the less God-conscious we become! We forget that God owns it all.

Even as a church, the further we get from our harsh realities, the less God-conscious we become. Remember the days before air conditioners and padded church pews? Remember the days before nursery, when there were twice as many babies as adults in services? Remember how long those services were? A tornado went through my hometown of Jackson, Tennessee, and people everywhere were getting together in church and praying—even people who hadn't been to church in years. Folks' houses were hanging up in trees, and the first thing they wanted to do was go to church! FEMA came through and gave them some extra money, they got their houses in place, and now they have no time for worship. They have no time for God consciousness! They forgot that God owns it all.

When the harsh realities of disaster set in, we are liable to start asking someone to pray for us. Could it be that God allows harsh realities to set in because He knows that we will forget about Him if it were not for those harsh realities? Indeed, that was the cycle of the Israelites. God blessed them. They worked hard in Egypt. They cried out to God. He gave manna from heaven. They ate, became fat, and ignored Him.

Will we do the same? We won't if we remember the first exercise to build economic strength: Recognize that God owns it all.

THOUGHT PROVOKERS

1. How much credit do you think is wise to take for your economic progression?

2. Do you recognize that your intelligence comes from God? When you have engaged in commerce, do you recognize that God has enabled your wealth?

3. How can you be content when you do not have as many resources as you desire or think you deserve?

Chapter 7

EXERCISE 2: SHOW ME THE MONEY

The second exercise that will help us to build economic strength is to account for all our resources so that nothing will be lost. Where did last year's money go? Where did this year's money go? Where will next year's money go? Money management is a sensitive issue, and it is also a spiritual issue, for Jesus mentioned money more often in His parables than any other subject (see Matthew 18:21-35, 19:16-26, 25:14-29). In fact, some people say that the Bible covers money more than any other topic.

Why is that? God knew that money would be an area of constant struggle for us where we would need constant direction. He knew we would struggle with debt. And as we will see in a later chapter, He also knew the power of debt to rule us and then ruin us.

What is the answer? Let us look at Jesus teaching the multitudes. Thousands of people—the Bible says 5,000 men—had followed Him until late in the evening. Naturally after hours of sitting on a hillside listening to Jesus, they were hungry. Imagine a mob of more than 5,000 starving people. Jesus fed them and then gathered up the leftovers. Jesus accounted for all His resources! The leftovers filled twelve baskets. What a lesson in frugality. We can learn a lot about managing our resources from this Bible account.

Jesus fed the people and took up the leftovers. What do we do with our leftovers? Do we know where all our "stuff" is? Do we have stuff in the basement that we know not of? Are we still buying more stuff to put into the basement on top of that other stuff?

We cannot manage what we do not perceptively see.

Jesus accounted for all His resources! After feeding thousands of people on a hillside, Jesus collected and counted the leftovers, and came up with twelve baskets full. If Jesus accounted for all His resources, what should we do? He is modeling economic management for us! He didn't waste anything. Imagine the garbage company stopping at Jesus' house. They would say, "That man doesn't ever have much garbage." He did not throw useful stuff away; He used it. We do not need to accumulate a lot of extra stuff. We do need to use all that we have and to manage it well.

We cannot manage what we do not perceptively see. Imagine trying to supervise or manage people, but never knowing who they are. We cannot possibly manage them! We do not know where they are, who they are, or how many of them there are. We cannot manage what we cannot perceptively see! We can only manage the resources of which we have conscious awareness. We cannot manage resources that are on the outside of our conscious awareness.

Some people have hidden money and forgotten where they hid it. Or they have lost money. It is impossible to manage lost or misplaced money. Others have missed important purchases because they did not know that they could afford to purchase them; that is the flip side of not knowing how much money we have. We may have skipped lunch because we forgot that we had stashed money in the glove box of the car. We cannot manage what is outside our perceptive vision. We cannot manage what we cannot see. Therefore, we must account for all our resources.

MAKING AN ACCOUNT

We can't take a journey unless we know where we are starting and where we're going. So in order to make the move from financial stress to financial stability to financial strength, we have to begin by taking a good long look at where we are and determine how we got there, for that is the only way we will move on (and move up). The first step toward wise resource management is to account for our resources so that nothing will become lost. If we expect God to multiply our resources, we must know what we have before we start, and what we have when we finish.

As we have seen, Jesus was a man with unlimited resources, yet He did not waste leftovers. He accounted for all His resources! Jesus is modeling economic management for us! If Jesus accounted for all His resources, what should we do? We should manage our resources and manage them well. We cannot manage what we cannot see. We cannot manage resources of which we do not have any conscious awareness. We must focus our way towards financial freedom. We must perceptively see where we are. So the first order of resource management is to make an accounting of what we have (and what we don't have, that is, debt that we owe to others).

My counseling experiences tell me that most people over-estimate their income and underestimate their outgo. An excellent way to show us the big picture is to take the next 100 days and keep a written record of 100 percent of our income and outgo. If we pick up a penny on the street, we should add that to our income. If we spend seventy-five cents for coffee, we should write it down as an expense. We should note the source of all income and the purpose for each expense—doing it each day, not at the end of the month. Then at the end of the 100 days, we can take a backward look and discover where our money went (see Matthew 25:14-25).

Tracking our finances on paper can be an eye-opener. It will show us our financial picture clearer by looking at it on paper. It will help us to learn where we are spending our money. What percentage of our money do we spend on utilities? When we figure that out, we might start turning out the lights when we leave a room. When we find out how much money we are spending on the water bill, we might stop taking 45-minute hot showers. We might speed up and scrub up and get out of the shower a lot faster.

The Financial Management Worksheet will give us a small picture of where our money is going. This tool will help us to make an account of our financial situation. It will help us to list every expense we have—the ones we think about and the ones we never think about. Take some time to work on this. Spouses should work on it together. Parents can involve their children in the process. (We will talk more in a later chapter about teaching our children to be good financial stewards, and this is an excellent way to begin.) Write directly in the book, or photocopy the form so that it can be updated regularly.

FINANCIAL MANAGEMENT WORKSHEET

INCOME (per month)
Income
    Salary   _____
    Other   _____
Total gross income   _____

EXPENSES (per month)
Non-discretionary expenses
1. **God's Kingdom** (offerings;
   should be a minimum of ten
   percent of gross income)   _____
2. **Man's kingdom** (taxes)   _____
3. **Savings** (should be a
   minimum of ten percent
   of net income)   _____

    Total non-discretionary
    expenses   _____

    Net spendable income
    (gross income minus non-
    discretionary expenses)   _____

Discretionary expenses
4. **Housing**
    Mortgage or rent   _____
    Insurance   _____
    Taxes   _____
    Electricity   _____
    Gas   _____
    Water   _____
    Telephone   _____
    Sanitation   _____
    Cable   _____

Maintenance/repair _____
Other _____
Total housing expense _____

5. Food _____

6. Transportation
Car/truck payments _____
Fuel _____
Insurance _____
License _____
Taxes _____
Maintenance/repair _____
Other _____
Total transportation expense _____

7. Insurance
Life _____
Medical _____
Other _____
Total insurance expense _____

8. Child care _____

9. Debt reduction (monthly payments)

Credit Card #1 _____
Credit Card #2 _____
Credit Card #3 _____
Credit Card #4 _____
Loan #1 _____
Loan #2 _____
Loan #3 _____
Other _____
Other _____
Total debt reduction _____

10. Clothing _____

11. Investments (monthly payments)
Savings #1 _____
Savings #2 _____
Savings #3 _____
Total investments _____

12. Health care
Medical _____
Dental _____
Eye care _____
Medications _____
Other _____
Other _____
Total health expenses _____

13. Recreation
Eating out _____
Trips _____
Babysitting _____
Movies _____
Activities _____
Vacation _____
Software, games, etc. _____
Other _____
Other _____
Other _____
Total recreation expenses _____

14. Miscellaneous
Pet care and supplies _____
Home computer
and supplies _____
Subscriptions _____
Gifts _____
Toiletries _____

Cosmetics _____
Cosmetology _____
Laundry _____
Detergent _____
Other cleaning supplies _____
Other _____
Other _____
Other _____
Total miscellaneous expenses _____

Total expenses _____

Income vs. Expenses

Net spendable income _____
Less expenses _____
Available money _____

AMOUNT OWED
15. Debt reduction

Credit Card #1 _____
Credit Card #2 _____
Credit Card #3 _____
Credit Card #4 _____
Loan #1 _____
Loan #2 _____
Loan #3 _____
Other _____
Other _____
Total debts _____

It may take us some time to put together an account of our financial picture—and what we see may shock us. Are our finances within focus? Too often our finances are out of focus and we do not want to know the real condition of them. We prefer to spend blindly. Some refuse to balance their check-book for fear of discovering that not enough money is in the account to cover the check that they want to write. They write the check and just hope it passes through the bank. That's a terrible way to live. We cannot get to financial freedom from there.

That is why it is critical to spend time working on our Financial Management Worksheet. Investing the time to do it is part of being good stewards of what God has given us. Once we take control of our finances, we will have peace and contentment that we have never experienced before. We may not be rich, but we will be in control, rather than letting our debts control us. And we will grow from financial stress to financial stability to financial strength. Wow, what a feeling!

THOUGHT PROVOKERS

1. When I tracked my expenses for 100 days, I was shocked to find _____.

2. When I filled out the Financial Management Worksheet, I was shocked to find _____.

3. Here are three things I can do to get control of my finances: _____, _____, _____.

Chapter 8

EXERCISE 3: ACT YOUR WAGE

The third exercise that will help us to build economic strength is to "act our wage." In other words, we must learn to live within our salary and other sources of income. In this chapter, we will learn how to spend wisely the money we have, establish a financial model, splurge (yes, there is a right way and a wrong way), and set up a system of accountability.

SPENDING WISELY

There is a wise way to spend, and a not-so-wise way. Here's an indicator that we are not spending well. If our spending habits change on payday, we are not doing well and we are a terrible manager of our resources. We should manage our money well enough so that people don't even know when we get paid. If we need (not want) to buy something, we can buy it on Tuesday, and not have to wait until payday.

This is a management issue, and we must learn to manage! Most people think their financial condition is because they do not have not enough income—but the problem is not the amount that is coming in, but the amount we are letting go out. It is crucial not only to receive enough money, but also to disburse it in a manner that is acceptable. One of the best ways to do this is to establish a financial model. There are many sound financial models to choose from, and we must find the one that best accommodates our income, expenditures, and dispositions. Below are some examples. If we are married, we should take time with our spouse to discuss the various models and find the one that is acceptable to both. If we are single, we must go through the same process and find the model that works best for our circumstances. If the model fails to accommodate our needs, we can adjust it or adopt another model that will. Here are some financial models from which to choose:

1. One spouse pays all the expenditures for the entire family from his or her income, while the other spouse accountably saves and invests his or her total income.

2. One spouse pays all the expenditures for the entire family, while the other spouse accountably saves and invests a portion of his or her income.

3. One spouse pays all the expenditures for the entire family, while the other spouse unaccountably spends.

4. One spouse assumes responsibility for scheduled and recurring expenditures, while the other spouse assumes responsibility for accidental, incidental, and non-recurring expenditures.

5. Family expenditures are divided into two categories; each spouse assumes total responsibility for one category.

6. All income is deposited into one account. One spouse maintains custody. All expenditures are governed by the jurisdiction of that custodial spouse.

7. All income is deposited into one account. Both husband and wife corroborate on every expenditure.

8. All income is deposited into one account. Husband and wife corroborate on every expenditure that exceeds a preset spending limit.

9. All income is deposited into one account. Husband and wife designate certain categories of expenses to be paid automatically, but corroborate on every other expenditure.

10. Each spouse retains an agreed-upon percentage or amount of his or her income to keep for personal designated

items; all remaining income is jointly held and allocated only after corroboration of both husband and wife.

Once we decide on a financial model, we must learn how to spend wisely the money we have. The first spending items on the Financial Management Worksheet that we compiled in the previous chapter are called "non-discretionary" expenses, meaning they are non-negotiable. First is spending (or investing) part of our resources in God's Kingdom. We will talk more about this in later chapters, but our offerings to God's Kingdom should be a minimum of ten percent of our gross income. Next is what we pay "man's kingdom," otherwise known as taxes, and then what we pay ourselves, otherwise known as savings. It is very tempting to put this off by saying, "I will start saving money when I start making more money"—but that is not human nature. We must force ourselves to get into the habit of saving money. If we can save when we are making a little money, we will learn the discipline so that when we are making a lot of money we will save even more (instead of spending it all). We will look more at savings in a later chapter.

The key to making a financial model work is that we should never spend all we receive. Many people plan to spend all they have. Let's say we are supposed to get a $5 raise, but even before we get it, we have already gone out and spent it in advance. Let me share a secret: It takes the accounting department about two months to get that raise into the system, so we have already spent money that we will not get for another two months. Now we've got a raise and we are in worse condition than we were before we got it! That is a terrible way to live. If we have it in our mind that we are planning to buy something when we get some money, we are in a dangerous predicament.

God wants us to budget our resources...

God wants us to budget our resources; we should allocate resources before we begin a project or make any purchase, and account for resources after we finish. Jesus knew what His resources were before He started to feed the thousands. They had five small barley loaves and two small fish (see John 6:1-9). Joseph knew how many resources he needed to complete his project. They needed twenty percent each year during seven years of plenty to cover seven years of famine (see Genesis 41:34-57).

We should also deliberately account for our resources after the project ends. Jesus knew how many resources were left after the project. They recovered twelve baskets of food (see John 6:12-13). The king knew how many resources were left.

They recovered the excess and used it to make more utensils for the house of the Lord (see 2 Chronicles 24:8-14).

One of the first places to start getting control of our resources is with the money that we spend on food. Most of us eat too much—not all, but most of us. And then we eat too much of the wrong and most expensive food. The products in those snack machines at work are too expensive and unhealthy. If we looked closely at one of those little packets and saw how much sodium was in there, we would never eat anything from a snack machine again! The cheapest and healthiest way to eat is cooking at home; then we definitely know what we are eating because we put it in there ourselves.

Accurately measure the value and worth of all prospective purchases. Buying an item on sale that will go unused is not a bargain at all; it is an expensive waste of God's resources. We need to obtain a good value for what God has given to us. We should not pay $10 for a $5 trinket that we are going to use. Nor should we pay $5 for a $10 trinket that we are not going to use. We must ask not only, "Is it worth it?" but also, "Is it worth it to me?" We may need to wait until the price goes down. When we count the cost of interest, we may conclude that we need to wait and pay cash. We should deliberately decide when and where we are going to spend our resources (which are God's resources). We may need to purchase something else before we purchase what we really want.

We should deliberate at least twenty-four hours before purchasing unbudgeted items, discussing these expenditures with our spouse. Is this a necessary item? Is it something we need, or something we want? If it is something we want, and the money is not there to purchase it, we need to rethink the purchase.

If we still have difficulty, then perhaps we need to stay away from places that tempt us to spend money. If our weakness is clothing, stay away from the malls. If our weakness is our computer, stay away from the software or game store. If our weakness is crafts, stay out of the craft shops. We should also not shop with (and perhaps even stay away from) people who tempt us to spend money we don't have, people who overspend, people who can afford to spend more than we do, or people we feel a need to impress. If friends admire and compliment our purchases when they know we cannot afford them, they are not friends. We may need to tell them honestly and forcefully that we are trying to live within our budget and get out of debt; it may humble us, but it will ultimately help us. (And it may help them, too, if they are in the same situation.)

We should also avoid situations that tempt us to spend. We shouldn't go shopping when we are ill prepared financially, haven't balanced our checkbook, or have bills that we haven't received or paid. We also shouldn't go shopping when we are ill prepared physically (tired or hungry), or emotionally (depressed, etc.). Buying something when we have been led onto an emotional plateau by a member of the opposite sex is risky and foolish. Sales persons are trained to convince us that our self-esteem will improve if we only buy this lipstick or that car. Sex sells.

SPLURGING

A good reason to plan our spending is so that we have some money left over to splurge. If we don't have any money left over, we can't splurge. Many people get into trouble splurging. There is a proper and an improper way to splurge. It is fine to splurge, but we must learn to do it right. We must learn how to splurge.

Let's say that we get paid on Friday. On Friday evening, we pay all the bills, and we have $100 left over, so we go out and splurge. Now that sounds good. All the bills are paid, and we have some money left over, and we know we will get paid next Friday. It looks like we're okay. We're okay on Monday and on Tuesday. On Wednesday, we run over a piece of glass and destroy a $125 tire. Here we are making $75,000 a year and can't buy a tire for our car! That is bad management. What got us into trouble? We should have splurged with the money that we had left over from the previous payday, not the current one.

Let's suppose we get paid on Sunday. We had $50 left over from our past pay period and we are getting paid today. We should splurge only with a portion of the $50. If we splurge before our next pay period with what we just got paid, we are saying, "I know that no emergencies are going to arise"—but they always arise! Splurge with no more than half the money that has been left over from the pay period before the last one. Let's suppose a family had $100 left over. They splurged away $75 on Saturday. A family with $25 left over may seem good. Unfortunately, what will happen if they have to make an emergency trip to the doctor, costing $50? Now the $100 surplus has eroded into a $25 deficit. Splurge, but splurge wisely.

ACCOUNTABILITY

Another way to be a wise steward of the resources that God has given us is to become accountable to a responsible person. If we make twice as much as we did five years ago and are ten times further in debt, we need to let somebody help us. Most people will do better with their money if somebody is peeking over their shoulders. It's just the nature of who we are. We tend to do better when we know we will have to explain our actions to someone else. This applies to management of our time, finances, or any other resources we may have. There is no shame in letting someone help us. In fact, the more dire our financial situation, the more accountability we need. It may take some humility to ask someone to help us, and to show them the figures in the preceding chapter, but in the long run we will be better off.

If we knew someone was going to look at all our financial dealings, there are some things we wouldn't do because they are not wise. Every person will strive to do better when someone manages them—when they are accountable to another. Many families are in a bad financial state because of one of the members of that household. Someone in that house keeps saying, "I'm going to spend"—and they don't have a clue what they are doing. They have been messing up the family for years. They ought to let somebody help them. By becoming accountable to someone else, it will force them to discipline themselves and manage their resources better.

One spouse may wish to be accountable to the other. Families will usually handle their resources more conservatively when they are accountable to each other. The Bible advocates mutual accountability: "Be subject to one another in the fear of Christ" (Ephesians 5:21). This will prevent one spouse from buying something without consulting the other, slipping it into the house, and hiding it, later to say, "I have had this for a while." How ungodly and unfortunate to set such an example for their children.

Or it may be wise to choose someone outside the family. A good person to be accountable to is a mature person who has achieved economic contentment. Many, if not all, successful companies operate with multiple minds reviewing especially sizeable outlays of cash. A comptroller or accountant may even scrutinize expenditures made by the owner.

This chapter gives us some specific things to do to "act our wage" and begin to take control of our finances. None of these things is easy. In fact, taking control of our finances can be challenging because it requires us to change the way we do things. If we are serious about being good stewards of the resources that God has given us, we may have to change some habits. To change a habit, we must change what we do every day. We can't change habits by changing something once a month or once a week. We have to change it every day.

Remember, our goal is to move from financial stress to financial stability to financial strength. It's a good feeling when we go to the mailbox, find some bills, and know that we have enough money to pay them the day they come. That takes the stress off us. We may decide to wait closer to the due date, but we know that we have the money to pay them the day they come. It is stressful when the bill comes and the due date is before our pay date. God doesn't want us to live like that. We *can* move from financial stress to financial stability to financial strength. Acting our wage will help us to do that.

THOUGHT PROVOKERS

1. What surprised you about your income and outgo? What didn't surprise you?

2. Where do you need to make changes? What changes could you make? Think about the pros and cons of each option. Is not making any change an option? What would be the consequence?

3. Would having an accountability partner help you? What friend or family member could you ask to fill this role?

Chapter 9

EXERCISE 4: ESCAPE THE DEBT TRAP

The fourth exercise that will help us to build economic strength is to escape the debt trap. If we are in debt, we must make a plan to get out of debt. If we are not in debt, we must make a commitment not to get into it.

God chose to communicate truths to His people through Solomon, the wisest and wealthiest man who ever lived. When the wisest and wealthiest man who ever lived speaks about money, we ought to listen. Here is one of the great truths he gave us: "The rich rules over the poor, and the borrower becomes the lender's slave" (Proverbs 22:7). This should not be a foreign concept to us, but God already told us earlier in the Scriptures that He wants His people to be rich and not poor, to be the lender and not the borrower: "For the

Lord your God will bless you as He has promised you, and you will lend to many nations, but you will not borrow; and you will rule over many nations, but they will not rule over you" (Deuteronomy 15:6). God emphasized His intentions for His people in other verses, such as Deuteronomy 28:1-14.

God's preferred state for His people is to be rich and not poor, lenders and not borrowers.

God's preferred state for His people is to be rich and not poor, lenders and not borrowers. Yet where are we? We are a church in debt. We are a church filled with members who are in debt. Debt is a part of our lives. And with it comes bondage. Jesus wants to be lord of every aspect of our life, but if debt rules, then debt has dethroned Him. Debt has pushed Jesus off the throne. Debt has become our king.

We may think that Jesus is lord of our life, but how many decisions have we made that we would not have made if we had not been in debt? "I hated to do that, but I owed." "I would have never refinanced my house at a higher interest rate, but I owed." "I never would have taken out a second mortgage, but I needed to pay off the car." "I would have never done that if I did not have to get my son out of jail."

If we have made any decision because of debt, then who rules in our life? Who is lord of our life—Jesus or debt? Debt brings bondage. Debt rules. Who do we want to rule over us—Jesus or debt? Jesus gives us marching orders, but before we can carry them out, we have to consult with our debt. Who rules? Debt rules. If debt is ruling in our life, then Jesus is no longer the lord of our life.

If we must consult with debt before we make decisions, it is likely that debt is ruling in our affairs. And after debt has ruled for a while, debt then ruins. Many people find themselves doing things that they would never do if it were not for debt. People who get into debt often try to get out in a hurry by stealing something, selling something, or other illegitimate means. Often they are caught and trapped in the prison system. They then want to cry "foul." Indeed, debt rules and then debt ruins.

Debt has ruined many lives. The lives of many people are messed up because debt has stressed them out. Debt breeds contempt for God. Debt is a terrible enemy. It will cause us to disregard God and determine to increase our income. It will cause us to look God in the face and say, "I don't care what You say. I'm going to do this anyway." Debt will cause us to have a standoff with God, to oppose and resist Him. It is a terrible enemy because it will cause us to have a bad attitude about God. It will cause us to say, "I know that God said it, but it doesn't matter what He said. I need more money in this house, so I will buy this lottery ticket." Debt will cause us to say, "I know I ought to go to church, but I need more money in this house, so I'm going to take a Sunday part-time job."

Debt rules and ruins as it causes us to have contempt for God. Recently a policeman was arrested for bank robbery. Why? He explained his actions by saying one of his businesses was suffering and he needed the money. Isn't that amazing? He had a job and a business, and he still had to rob banks! Something is wrong with that picture!

Debt will cause us to disregard God in an effort to decrease our expenses. Debt will cause us to look God in the face and say, "I know what God says, but I've got to cut back on my expenditures. I know that I ought to go to Kroger and buy my groceries, but they are selling meat at half price on the corner." Debt will cause us not to ask where that half-price meat comes from. Debt will cause us to buy illegal food stamps so that we can save half price on our groceries. Debt will cause otherwise honest people to be dishonest.

Debt will cause us to sell marijuana, to look the other way when our children are doing things that are illegal, to cheat on our taxes, to lie about our income, and fill out false time cards. Debt rules and debt ruins. No wonder God wants His people to stay out of debt. God doesn't want His people in bondage. He does not want His people ruled by debt. He wants to keep Jesus on His throne.

Whenever I meet people who are more than eighty years of age and healthy, I want to know how they did it. I have found only one consistent thing: They managed their debt well. Isn't that amazing? It is not surprising, however, because debt generates physical frustration. The stress of three jobs causes physical frustration. Debt generates emotional frustration. When we are in debt, our subconscious never forgets it. While we sleep at night, our subconscious tries to figure out how to pay the bills. No wonder when we wake in the morning we are tired. While we sleep, our subconscious mind is working overtime. Making monthly payments on a television that has long ago been sold at the pawn shop is no fun. Making monthly payments on a car when we do not have enough money to repair it in order to drive it is painful.

Debt can cause health problems. We may have a splitting headache (possibly caused by the stress of debt) and do not feel like going to work. The thought occurs to us to call in sick so that we don't have to go to work, but as we look out the window, our car says, "You better get up and go to work and pay for me, or I will be parked elsewhere." We look across the room and our Plasma screen television set says, "You better get up and get out of here, or you will be home alone." Debt does not care how bad our head hurts.

Debt can also cause marital problems. Debt contributes to the conflict between most husbands and wives. There is either too little money or a difference of opinion about how to spend the money.

Debt generates physical frustration, emotional frustration, marital frustration, and spiritual frustration. It is difficult to sing, " Oh, how I love Jesus" when our bills are months behind. It is difficult to sing, "Send the light" when we are unsure if our utilities will remain turned on. Debt can become a terrible monster.

Debt assumes something about the future. When we go into debt, we are assuming that somewhere in the future we are going to do business and make a profit. We are depending on a future over which we have no control! Who controls the future? God! Therefore, when we go into debt, we are depending on Him. We are obligating God and we should not do that without His permission!

> Come now, you who say, "Today or tomorrow we will go to such and such a city, and spend a year there and engage in business and make a profit." Yet you do not know what your life will be like tomorrow. You are just a vapor that appears for a little while and then vanishes away. Instead, you ought to say, "If the Lord wills, we will live and also do this or that" (James 4:13-15).

Debt assumes that we will engage in commerce in the future to the extent that we will gain a profit. It is God who gives us the power to gain wealth. "But you shall remember the Lord your God, for it is He who is giving you power to make wealth, that He may confirm His covenant which He swore to your fathers, as it is this day" (Deuteronomy 8:18). Therefore, we must consult with Him ahead of time. Before we go into debt, we should pray about it. Ask God's permission, and until He gives us some indication that it is all right to go into debt, we should not do so. Is it the Lord's will to charge another big-screen television on our credit card when we have two already and we don't have time to watch either of them? Is it the Lord's will to charge a microwave oven at Sears? We need to have answers to those questions, because we are obligating God, and we never ought to obligate Him without His permission.

Debt repayment revolves around a spiritual principle. Do not accumulate more indebtedness than we can comfortably repay. Use credit wisely. Remember the little thing called interest. It increases the amount that we must repay. Interest is not interesting to the borrower. It is interesting only to the lender. Car salesmen, for example, sell monthly payments. They usually do not sell the total amount. When we are considering buying a car, we need to know how much the total cost of the car will be, including interest. How much will the insurance and maintenance cost? All of these items and more are part of the expense package.

If we are already in debt, we must repay it! Our credit-card purchases are not gifts from VISA or MasterCard. Neither does

Sears or J. C. Penney give us those items. When we take out a loan, they are not giving us the merchandise for free. Our Lord says that we must repay those debts. "The wicked borrows and does not pay back, but the righteous is gracious and gives" (Psalm 37:21). Debt must be repaid. Refusing to pay indebtedness exposes the character flaw of wickedness. Readily paying indebtedness exposes the character trait of righteousness.

We need to know what we owe and to whom we owe it. We need to know the "what" and the "where" of our indebtednesses. Then, if we cannot pay our creditors by the day in which we have promised to pay them, we must contact them and make alternate payment arrangements. We owe them an explanation and an alternate arrangement! We must not hide from our creditors. If we have agreed to pay our Sears credit card by the eighth of the month, we should pay it so that Sears will have their money credited to our account by the eighth. We should not mail our payment on the eighth.

We must not only pay something on our debts, but we must pay more than the monthly addition of interest. If our debts are overwhelming and beyond our handling, there are services available to help us. We can contact our local consumer credit counseling agency and they will help us renegotiate with our creditors.

There is no free ride. Eventually, we must pay for all of our credit purchases. Now, when we say "charge it," we must remember that we must pay it later. We must pay our bills. We must repay what we have agreed to repay.

Money management is as much an attitude as an amount. The proper attitude will move us from financial stress to financial stability, and from financial stability to financial strength. The proper attitude will also enable us to help move someone else along the path toward financial strength. We can never fulfill our God-given assignment unless we manage our money—and that means getting out of debt and staying out of debt.

THOUGHT PROVOKERS

1. How has your view of debt changed as a result of reading this chapter?

2. What does this statement mean to you personally: "If I am in debt, then debt, not Jesus, is lord of my life." Where has debt affected your life? Your spouse's life? Your children's lives?

3. What changes do you need to make? List three things you can do today. Will you do them?

Chapter 10

EXERCISE 5: SOW TO THE HARVEST

The fifth exercise that will help us to build economic strength is to sow, or give, to the harvest. What happens if we jump off the top of a ten-story building onto a concrete sidewalk? The force of gravity will propel us downward, the impact with the concrete will crush us, and we will experience much pain. God placed the law of gravity within the universe. Life progresses more successfully when we cooperate with that law rather than violate it.

God gave us other laws, which always produce specified results. One of those is the law of the harvest. God placed within the universe the law of the harvest. Just as there are benefits to following the law of gravity, life progresses more successfully when we cooperate with and not violate the law of the harvest. When we give, we cooperate with the law of the harvest. When we give, we also cooperate with other laws. One is the law of implantation, which says that in order to harvest, we must first plant, for nothing is harvested where no seed has been sown. We can never reap before planting (see John 4:35-38), but we can always reap after planting.

When we give, we cooperate with the law of identification, which says that we harvest in like kind to the seed that was sown. We harvest the same quality (see Galatians 6:7), but we harvest beyond the quantity that we plant (see Luke 6:38). When we give, we cooperate with the law of incubation, which says that what is planted needs time to germinate, grow, and come to fruition (see Galatians 6:6-10, Ecclesiastes 11:1). When we give, we cooperate with the law of intensification, which says that what is planted yields more than the seed planted (see 2 Corinthians 9:6-12). When we give, we should sow expecting a harvest (see Philippians 4:15-19).

We have already seen that God has established His ownership of all the earth, yet He has chosen to depend upon His people to finance the work of His Kingdom on earth. God chose to wait upon the stewardship of His people to advance the work of His Kingdom. He has given His people an awesome privilege and responsibility. Shortly after the Israelites crossed the Red Sea, God gave them an opportunity to participate in a fundraising campaign to build the tabernacle, a place of worship (see Exodus 25:1-8). They success-fully responded to the challenge (see Exodus 36:7).

We now have an opportunity to participate in the advancement of God's Kingdom, and many will respond to the call and be successful at it. The ones who participate are those who have it in their hearts to do so (see Exodus 35:5, 21-22, 26, 29) as well as those who have it in their hands (see Exodus 35:23-25).

Through the Old Testament, God provided valuable infor-mation for New Testament believers (see Romans 15:4) about the law of the harvest. From the successful fundraising campaign in Exodus, we can learn valuable principles for our own capital fundraising. We discover the root of the generosity of those who contributed resources for the building the tabernacle. God depended upon those whose heart was willing (see Exodus 25:1-2). Their hearts were willing because the book of the covenant and the blood of the covenant had conditioned their hearts (see Exodus 24:7, 25:8). We also discover the reason for the generosity of those who contributed resources for building the tabernacle. They recog-nized God's ownership of the resources before the construc-tion of the tabernacle and after the construction of the taber-nacle (see Exodus 25:1-2, 8).

Jesus told a parable of a rich man who fired his manager for mismanagement (see Luke chapter 16). To gain the favor of the rich man's debtors, the manager reduced the amount that each debtor owed (see verses 3-7). When he saw what happened, the rich man praised his manager for behaving so shrewdly (see verse 8a), yet in spite of the praise of the owner, Jesus said nothing positive about the manager's behavior. Instead, He contrasted the behavior of the people of satan and the people of God. He concluded that the people of satan behaved more advantageously toward each other than the people of God (see verse 8b). Jesus referred to their wealth as the wealth of unrighteousness (see verse 9b). Money is morally neutral, but the monetary system was morally corrupt.

Jesus encouraged His disciples to obey the law of the harvest and use their wealth for eternal purposes (see verse 9). Our earthly use of wealth affects us eternally. What impact does our use of wealth have upon us? Let us consider the consequences as we examine Jesus' sermons on wealth. Those who use money wisely are promoted to eternity (see verses 10-13). Jesus spoke of others who used wealth wisely, such as the good Samaritan (see Luke 10:30-37). Those who use money unwisely are demoted to eternity (see Luke 16:19-31). Others failed to use wealth wisely (see Luke 12:13-22).

The apostle Paul gave of his wisdom (see Acts 20:17-21, 31). He also gave of his wealth (see Acts 20:34-35a). He then reminded the elders of the church of the words of Jesus, who had pronounced a blessing upon those who would give (see

Acts 20:35b). This particular statement of Jesus is not found written within Scripture, but we know that Jesus said much that is unwritten (see John 20:30-31, 21:25).

God wants our wealth to make a positive difference.

God wants our wealth to make a positive difference. If we had less, what positive good would be neglected? If nothing, we are not using our wealth to its capacity. If we had more, what positive good would be done? If nothing, then we do not need more.

WATCHING THE WISDOM OF A WEALTHY WIDOW WOMAN

A little boy received two nickels from his mother. One nickel was for Sunday school and the other was for candy. On the way to church, the little boy kept flipping his nickel as he walked along the street, and he accidentally dropped it. He looked down as his shining nickel rolled right into a grate, then slowly looked skyward and said, "Lord, there goes Your nickel." Give to God first, not what is left over. Withholding from God stifles our growth (see Proverbs 11:24).

For the last incident in His public ministry, Jesus visited the temple, where He deliberately observed how both the rich and poor gave their financial contributions (see Mark 12:41-44). He evaluated their comparative contributions, then publicly reported His conclusions to His disciples. Later the Holy Spirit had His conclusions recorded for further public reporting. This proves that while giving may be a personal matter, it is not a private matter.

Jesus said that this widow had contributed more than all the other contributors. Did she give more in total amount? No, but she gave a greater percent of what she had. She gave 100 percent.

Disciple A has $1,000 and contributes $200. That's a twenty percent contribution ($200 divided by $1,000). Disciple B has $2,000 and contributes $300. That's a fifteen percent contribution ($300 divided by $2,000). Who has given a greater percent? Disciple A has, because even though the dollar amount he gave was smaller than Disciple B, Disciple A gave a greater percentage of what he had (twenty percent versus the fifteen percent that Disciple B gave).

We need to evaluate our own personal financial contribution. We need to know what percentage of God's money we are keeping and/or spending for ourselves or our families. We also need to know what total amount of God's money we are keeping and/or spending for ourselves (family).

The widow also gave a greater amount because of what she had left after she gave. She had nothing left. Disciple A, who had $1,000 and contributed $200, had still $800 left. Disciple B, who had $2,000 and contributed $300, still had $1,700. Who has more money left? Disciple B did, even though he gave the greater dollar amount.

We must determine the percentage of our gross income that we are keeping and/or spending for ourselves, then we should divide our total monthly contribution by our total monthly income. We should also determine the total amount of our gross income that we are keeping and/or spending for ourselves, and then subtract our total monthly contribution from our total monthly income. One rule of thumb to follow is that after expenses for food and shelter, we should never spend more on anything than we contribute to God's Kingdom. I would not, for example, spend more on a vacation, hobby, or car than I give to the harvest.

In an effort to deny that God concerns Himself with amount, some have argued that a little given with the proper attitude is better than much given with an improper attitude. My suggestion is to give much with the proper attitude. Nothing in the Scripture verses we have looked at here addresses attitude. It never suggests that the rich had an improper attitude. Jesus addressed only the amount they gave, not their attitude.

We must determine that we will regularly and generously sow into God's harvest. Happiness requires more than just money. Whatever God blesses us with, we should invest a portion within the kingdom of God. Whatever monies we obtain, we should decide what investment we will make in the kingdom of God (see Proverbs 3:9-10). Solomon, the wisest man to live, understood the advantage of giving to the Lord. We can learn from him and never be too stingy to give to God.

THOUGHT PROVOKERS

1. Do you believe you must honor natural laws? Have you stopped to consider that you must learn and honor economic law?

2. Why would Jesus encourage His people to know and honor economic laws?

3. How important is it to know and understand that you must sow toward the harvest that you expect? What are some areas where you can begin sowing now?

Chapter 11

EXERCISE 6: SAVE FOR THE FUTURE

The sixth exercise that helps us to build economic strength is to save for the future. The future is always uncertain. The future is always filled with unexpected expenses. We must prepare for the future.

We have all heard stories about a great-grandma, who washed clothes and cleaned houses for $5 a week, died, and left tens of thousands of dollars to her church or favorite charity. How then is it that many people today who earn thousands of dollars per month cannot keep up with their bills? How did great-grandma save all that money? She did it by consistent discipline. She did it by not looking at what her neighbors had. She did not focus on what she did not have. She knew what was important. She knew that a sacrifice was necessary for her to honor the wisdom of the wise man Solomon: "A good man leaves an inheritance to his children's children, and the wealth of the sinner is stored up for the righteous" (Proverbs 13:22). The amount she saved did not depend on how much she earned, but rather on her attitude. She made a decision to be disciplined and not to spend everything she earned. Saving money is an attitude, not an amount. We, too, must make up our mind to start being disciplined.

No matter where we are with our financial resources—no matter what the bottom line on the Financial Management Worksheet in chapter seven—we must make the decision to start being disciplined and save a portion of what we earn or receive. We may be receiving unemployment benefits and feel that we cannot save a portion of that, but we must remember that saving money is an attitude, not an amount. Let's say our benefits had been $286 per week; now because of the economy the government made a decision to save *their* money by cutting all benefits by $6. What will we do? If we had made that same decision about the future of *our* money and saved that same $6, our attitude (and our financial circumstances) would be better. We would have had a small nest egg saved aside for emergencies such as this.

Young children should save a portion of their allowance or financial gifts they receive. College students can save a portion of what they make. Those working at McDonald's as their first job should learn to save something—no matter how small the amount—of every paycheck.

Financial management is an attitude.

Getting into the savings habit early in life will bear much fruit in later life. We cannot wait and say, "I'm going to start saving when I get to the next financial level," or we will never do it. For all we know the next financial level could be a step down, yet if we have been prudent by saving a portion of all that we earn or receive, an unforeseen financial setback will not set us back. Financial management is an attitude. If we don't have any money saved for emergencies, we don't have any business going to the movies. In fact, we can't afford to go to a movie. What happens if we're driving home from the movies and we run over a nail and blow out a tire? If we have money saved aside for an emergency, we have money to buy the tire. If we haven't saved, we charge it on our credit card, which incurs an additional fee and consequently we go further into debt. Saving money is a matter of discipline and is crucial to wise financial management.

Too many people believe that their financial predicament is due solely to their condition, but their financial predicament is more likely because they did not save in the first place. Through savings, Joseph saved Egypt from starvation and became renowned throughout all the world.

How we manage our money during every season and in every situation is as important as how much we receive. We must make the decision now to purposely and permanently save a portion of our income. We cannot wait until next year or next month or next paycheck. We must begin right now with a portion of our present income. It may be only $5 or $10 a paycheck, but the discipline of setting aside even that small amount will pay off later in life. If we are faithful to set aside a little, God will be faithful to give us even more to save.

We can start right now. We can check our pockets or purse. Instead of giving that change to the cashier so as not to break another dollar bill, we can put that change into a large container. We can have a container just for pennies, and another one for all other coins. Our financial increase can begin with as little as the change in our pockets or purse. This is an excellent exercise to help us build financial strength. "Work brings profit, but mere talk leads to poverty! Wealth is a crown for the wise; the effort of fools yields only folly" (Proverbs 14:23-24 NLT). If we begin to secure our future now, the future generations of our family will benefit.

THOUGHT PROVOKERS

1. How has your attitude about savings changed as a result of studying this chapter?

2. What does it mean to say that savings has more to do with attitude than with amount?

3. Where can you begin saving right now? What pleasures or luxuries are you indulging yourself that you could sell or stop using in order to save money?

Chapter 12

EXERCISE 7: TEACH OUR CHILDREN

T
he seventh exercise that helps to build our economic strength is to teach our children how to be good stewards of the resources that God has entrusted to them. As parents, it is our responsibility to teach our children not only table manners, dress codes, and respect for their elders, but also good fiscal discipline.

God assigned to fathers the responsibility of training their children in a specific way: "Fathers, do not provoke your children to anger, but bring them up in the discipline and instruction of the Lord" (Ephesians 6:4). Managing economic resources is part of the instructions of the Lord. Therefore, fathers must teach children how to manage money.

The Holy Spirit prohibited fathers, "Do not provoke your children." That literally means, "Do not anger your children to anger." In other words, out of our anger, we should not do what drives our children to anger—but does not all discipline anger children? Yes, but we should discipline our children so as to reinforce correct behavior rather than just retaliate against incorrect behavior. In the process of training our children, we should not anger them, but discipline them in their economic management—and reinforce that discipline.

The Holy Spirit solicited fathers to "bring them up in the training and instruction of the Lord." This means to educate children in all things, all the way to maturity. We should educate our children in the training of the Lord. Training includes both a verbal explanation and a visible demonstration that entices correct behavior. Therefore, fathers must demonstrate for their children the wise use of economic resources and do so in a way in which God approves. Fathers are not properly educating their children when they fail to demonstrate and explain the economic model that God approves.

God want parents to train their children to be rich and not poor, to be lenders and not borrowers.

"Train up a child in the way he should go, even when he is old he will not depart from it" (Proverbs 22:6). This verse is in the middle of a chapter on finances. So Solomon is really telling parents to train up their children in the way that they shall go with their finances. If we train them with good economic and fiscal responsibility habits, when they are older they will not depart from it. People have applied this verse to everything except what the Lord actually had in mind. It is clear from the context of the rest of the chapter that He wants parents to train their children in money management. God want parents to train their children to be rich and not poor, to be lenders and not borrowers. He knew that children would follow their parents' training in financial matters. As we have already seen throughout this book, it is difficult for us as adults to break ungodly financial habits. More often than not, we never outgrew our bad training on money matters. That cycle will continue if we do not train our children in the way they should go. Therefore, it is important for us to teach our children in the right way now, so that they will not get into the mess that some of us are in.

There are many ways we can do this. When Uncle Henry sends our children a birthday gift, we make them sit down and write him a thank-you note. Why? We want them to become trained to be gracious! If we give our children an allowance, we can take them through the same steps that we have followed in this book. Get out the calculator and put together a mini-financial management worksheet. Show them the lines for giving and saving, and come up with dollar amounts they will give and save each week. Give them a box to use as a bank and to save aside money for giving to God's harvest. Teach them how to spend wisely.

After we have shown them how to save a portion of what they've earned or received, then we should show them how to spend wisely what they have left. The next time we take them to the store, for example, we can show them how to compare prices and labels. We can use the Internet to show them how some clothes and foods are made by the same manufacturer, but have different labels—and that only the label and not the quality is what drives up the price of that item.

Depending on their age or level of understanding, we can tell them that they will have to pay a bill during a given month, rather than use their money for pleasure such as games or movies. We can teach them that God has given us as parents the responsibility to train them up in the way that they should go; all their resources are by means of God and that He is entrusting them to spend it wisely. I know from personal experience that there are times when children will not always listen to what we say; however for the most part, they never fail to imitate what we do. How many times did we say, "I'm never going to do what Daddy did"? Later in life, however, we end up doing exactly what he did; we imitated him. Since we know that, let's give our children something good and valuable to copy and take to their children and their children's children.

Showing our children how to acquire, save, and use money righteously is a good way to spend quality time with our children (see Deuteronomy 6:6-9.) What a wonderful heritage we will leave for our children if we can train them at an early age in sound financial management principles. What a legacy to teach children that debt will rule and ruin them—and that they never have to allow that to happen in their lives. They will never know financial stress, but will walk in financial stability and financial strength—once they commit and begin to change their perception about their finances. Many of us have prayed these things for our children and grandchildren, and we can be God's answers to our own prayers.

THOUGHT PROVOKERS

1. What values are you teaching your children when you buy them the latest expensive tennis shoes or jeans while you are living in an overcrowded apartment and don't have a car to drive to work?

2. If you give your children an allowance, what are some practical ways that you can teach them the value of earning a living?

3. How can you involve your children in your family finances? If money is tight, how can you explain to your children how it happened and how they can avoid the same plight? Does this take humility?

Chapter 13

PRIORITIES: THE URGENT OR THE IMPORTANT?

Many of us struggle with arranging our financial priorities. Do I pay this first? Do I pay that first? Do I do this first? Do I do that first? We are not the first people to have problems and struggles with our financial priorities. The Jews during the time of the prophet Haggai struggled to arrange their financial priorities. God provided help for them, and He will provide help for us to arrange our financial priorities.

When God delivered the Israelites from the land of Egypt and they arrived in the Promised Land, God required of them a "Sabbath year's rest" for the land. Every seven years, they were to allow the land to rest. They were not supposed to plant their fields or harvest their crop during that seventh year. That would be the equivalent to us working six years and taking a year off (see Exodus 23:10-11).

Now, the Jews had lived in the land of Canaan for 490 years and had never allowed the land to rest. They just went into Canaan and violated the command of God. For 490 years, they had walked in disobedience and in violation of the command of God! They had missed seventy Sabbath years. After they had been in the land of Canaan for 490 years, the Babylonian king, Nebuchadnezzar, came into the land, kidnapped the Jewish people, and took them to Babylon. For seventy years, they remained in Babylonian captivity.

God took His seventy years all at once! He asked them first and they didn't give, so He took all seventy years at once. God says, "You can do it the hard way, but I'm going to get My way." Always remember that. We can do it the easy way or the hard way, but God is going to get His way.

When the Israelites were released from Babylonian captivity, they were allowed to return to Jerusalem—and that is where Haggai picks up his message. When the Jews returned to Jerusalem from captivity, they started to rebuild the temple, rebuild the walls, and rebuild the city—but sixteen years after they returned, they stopped rebuilding the temple. So Haggai showed up on the scene and attempted to rekindle their memory and get the temple built.

Haggai told the people what the Lord had said. "This people," he began. Now, when a wife says to her husband, "Your son," immediately the husband knows that what is to follow is not good. When she says, "Our son," what is to follow is likely good. So when God says, "This people," what is to follow is not good. "Thus says the Lord of hosts, 'This people says, "The time has not come, even the time for the house of the Lord to be rebuilt"'" (Haggai 1:2).

The people replied that it was just not the time to build the house. So the Lord challenged their thinking (or lack of it). "Is it time to build your own houses?" He asked them. They were living in paneled houses while the house of the Lord lay in waste (see verses 3-4). Their homes had expensive cedars imported from Lebanon. Why wasn't it time to build the Lord's house? It seems as if they would have learned to arrange their financial priorities in a proper manner, but they still had not learned. Instead, their financial priorities violated the fundamental preferences of God. Haggai tried to get them to understand their sin. Wherever Abraham traveled, he always built an altar to God first. He recognized God's house before he built his own house.

God warned them that misplaced financial priorities would rob them of the blessings of God. When we are guilty of misplaced priorities, God allows our income to decrease. He did it then, and He will do it now. He will decelerate our income. "You have sown much, but harvest little; you eat, but there is not enough to be satisfied; you drink, but there is not enough to become drunk; you put on clothing, but no one is warm enough; and he who earns, earns wages to put into a purse with holes" (verse 6). They sowed much but harvested little. What happened? Their income went down.

Why? What happened? They placed themselves under a curse. "Therefore, because of you the sky has withheld its dew and the earth has withheld its produce. I called for a drought on the land, on the mountains, on the grain, on the new wine, on the oil, on what the ground produces, on men, on cattle, and on all the labor of your hands" (verses 10-11). A curse is a divine sentence of punishment that restricted and/or removed from someone or something the potential power to perform good (see Mark 11:12-14, 20-21). They planted, but God kept them from making money. Misplaced priorities reduced their income—and will reduce ours.

When we are guilty of misplaced priorities, God also increases our expenses. That is a terrible position to be in when our income goes down and our expenses go up. That scenario quickly stretches us beyond our means. That is what happened to the Israelites. God accelerated their output (see Haggai 1:6). We can never fill a container that leaks as fast as we fill it. God blew away their resources, and will do the same for us.

Just as a car mechanic uses symptoms to diagnose the problem of an automobile, symptoms in our life indicate what our problems may be. Often our economic increase fails due to spiritual drought. Here are several symptoms. We seek pleasure, but are never satisfied (see verse 6). Why? We are under the curse. We seek praise, but are never satisfied. Why" We are under the curse. We seek possessions, but we are never satisfied. Why? Again, we are under the curse.

Many of us earn more money than we ever imagined we would earn. We thought if we could make this much money we could be so happy, yet we have discovered that it didn't materialize. The rich ruler had much, yet a void existed within him. Therefore, he came to Jesus and inquired about eternal life. Afterwards, he went away sorrowful. How sad. He exchanged a long-term relationship with God for temporary wealth.

Earthly wealth minus God equals eternal poverty. Who fails to realize this equation? Jesus called them fools. Let us consider the persons who fail to realize this as we examine Jesus' sermon on fools (see Luke 12:13-21). Someone in the crowd asked Jesus to speak to a brother about a family inheritance dispute. Likely, greed had been the root cause of the dispute. Jesus excused Himself from participating, and instead warned them to be on guard against every form of greed (see verses 14-15a). He also informed them that life consisted of more than the abundance of possessions. He illustrated this point using the parable of the rich man (see verses 16-21). This man had lived as if life consisted of the abundance of his possessions, but Jesus called him a fool.

Fools fail to realize that earthly wealth minus God equals eternal poverty. They tell themselves how much they own (see verse 19b). They tell themselves how long they will own it (see verse 19c). God, on the other hand, tells them how little they own and how little time they have to own it: "You fool! This very night your soul is required of you; and now who will own what you have prepared?" (verse 20 NAS; see also James 4:14-15).

I do not ever want to hear Jesus refer to me as a fool because of the way I mishandled His resources (or for any other reason). We do not have to hear that. He loves us intensely, and He has given us His Word to instruct us how to be wise stewards, how to take control of our finances, and how to experience financial freedom.

Will you make the commitment today to do that?

God wants you to manage your finances by faith.

Your faith should govern your attitudes and actions toward money. Financial transactions are faith experiences. Your faith should govern the manner in which you acquire and manage money. Then money will never become your goal, god, or guide. Anxiety over financial matters will vanish.

God wants you to manage your finances by faith. Before you engage in a financial transaction, make sure that your faith governs it. Manage all the receiving of economic resources by faith. Manage all distributions of economic resources by faith. Real faith will not allow you to purchase a lottery ticket or participate in other thieveries. Faith will never allow you to write a bad check nor fill out an application for another credit card when you cannot pay for the ones you now have.

When faith governs your finances, flesh will not jeopardize your economic stability. When faith governs your finances, you will build economic strength. You will make the extraordinary move from financial stress to financial stability to financial strength. It is a move you will never regret making. God promises to send His Holy Spirit to instruct you, to guide you, and to encourage you along that path. Will you make the commitment to begin that journey today?

THOUGHT PROVOKERS

1. How do financial expenditures become faith experiences?

2. How can you help others to better prioritize their financial spending?

3. As you have read this chapter, what priorities are misaligned in your life? What do you need to do to get them back in proper order?

FOR THE
RECORD

Within Scripture, a distinct organism called the church existed. *Before* the death, burial, and resurrection, of Jesus Christ, Scripture declared that the church *would* come into existence (see Matthew 16:17-18). *After* the death, burial, and resurrection of Jesus Christ, Scripture declared that the church had *already* come into existence (see Acts 8:1-3).

The preaching of the death, burial, and resurrection of Jesus Christ resulted in people becoming forgiven of sins (see Acts 2:36-38). The preaching of the death, burial, and resurrection of Jesus Christ resulted in people becoming saved (see Acts 2:47). The preaching of the death, burial, and resurrection of Jesus Christ resulted in people becoming members of the church (see Acts 2:47).

Becoming forgiven of sins is equivalent to becoming saved, which is equivalent to becoming a member of the church. Those who are forgiven have become saved. Those who are saved are members of the church. One cannot become a member of the church without becoming saved. One cannot become saved without becoming a member of the church. So, to be saved is to be in the church, and to be in the church is the same as being saved.

The church, the body of Christ, came to exist only after the resurrection of Jesus. Christianity rises and/or falls on the resurrection of Jesus. The resurrection is more than a contemporary Easter idea; it is the very essence of Christianity. Christians pledge themselves not to a festive holiday program, but to a person, the resurrected Lord Jesus Christ.

The message of the death, burial, and resurrection of Jesus brought the church into existence. An appropriate response of faith toward the death, burial, and resurrection of Jesus brings a person into a forgiven state, saved, and into the church.

Believing that Jesus is the Christ, the Son of God, is an adequate response of faith. The death, burial, and resurrection of Jesus proves that He is the Christ, the Son of God (see Romans 1:1-4, Acts 17:30-31). Therefore, only those who believe can become forgiven of sins, saved, and members of the church (see John 8:24, Acts 4:1-4, 8:35-37).

Repenting of sin is an adequate response of faith. Repentance is the change of heart within a person (see

Matthew 21:28-32). In repentance, you change your allegiance (see Acts 2:38, 17:30, 26:19-20). You remove your
allegiance to your selfish self and pledge your allegiance
to the Savior.

Becoming baptized is an adequate response of faith.
Baptism is your response to the call of God (see 1 Peter
3:21). Near the beginning of his ministry, the apostle Peter
preached about baptism. Near the end of his ministry, the
apostle Peter wrote about baptism. Even now baptism
saves. What is baptism?

First we consider the dry side of baptism. It is a
response of the mind, for it is an internal appeal toward
God. The dry side is a response of the conscience. The
conscience is a product of accepted teachings (see John
8:1-9, Leviticus 20:10). The dry side is a response of a
good conscience. Within this context, a good conscience
is a heart that trusts in the resurrection of Jesus Christ (see
1 Peter 3:21). The resurrection proves that Jesus is the son
of God (see Romans 1:4, Acts 17:31). Only those who
believe in the resurrection of Jesus have a good
conscience for baptism (see John 8:24, Acts 8:35-37). If
your conscience is insufficiently taught, your conscience
will be insufficiently developed. And if your conscience is
incorrectly taught, then it will be incorrectly developed.

Baptism takes place while the penitent believer is in
water (see Acts 8:36-39). Baptism consists of taking the
penitent believer to the water, and never bringing the

water to the penitent believer. We should never attempt to reduce baptism to sprinkling and pouring of water. Some object to the necessity of being covered in water, but Jesus was sealed in His tomb (see Matthew 27:62-64, Romans 6:4). Some object to the necessity of water, yet water is specifically mentioned (see Acts 8:36-39, 10:47, 1 Peter 3:20-21). God refused to heal Naaman until he went into the water (see 2 Kings 5:14).

When those who heard the gospel believed, repented, and became baptized, they were forgiven, saved, and became a member of the church. Even now, a faith response to the death, burial, and resurrection of Jesus Christ allows one to become forgiven of sins, saved, and a Christian.

How much must one know before becoming baptized? I favor teaching an abundance of truth, yet we must ask, how much does the Scripture indicate that believers knew before they became baptized? How can we know how much a person knows? We know how much a person knows only by how much they indicate that they know. How much did early believers indicate they knew before being baptized? They indicated only that they believed that Jesus was the son of God (see Acts 8:37).

Believers need to know how to worship, where to worship, the nature of the church, and how to behave as a Christian, yet early believers were never called upon to demonstrate that level of knowledge prior to becoming baptized. Saying that one has become a Christian differs from saying that one has learned how to behave as a Christian (see Matthew 28:18-20). Some have become Christians, yet are worshipping in error. We must call them out of all religious error.

Who can baptize? The status of the one who teaches and baptizes has no effect upon the resulting state of the penitent believer. If it did, believers would be held responsible for what they could not possibly know, for no person can really know the heart of another.

Where must one be baptized? One can be baptized any place there is adequate water for a burial. Remember that only those who have believed, repented, and become baptized have become forgiven of sins, saved, and a member of the church. Nevertheless, all those who have believed, repented, and become baptized have become forgiven of sins, saved, and a member of the church.

Why is there so much confusion on subject of baptism? An intellectual exegesis of Scripture (bringing out of the text the ideas of the author) rather than an emotional exegesis of Scripture (bringing into the text the ideas of the reader) peels away most of the layers of confusion. The Holy Spirit could not come until after Jesus had risen from the dead and ascended to heaven (see John 16:7). Some forty days after Jesus had risen from the dead, the Holy Spirit was yet to come (see Acts 1:1-8). The Holy Spirit came on the day of Pentecost (see Acts 2:1-4). The Holy

Spirit revealed the message of truth to those who wrote Scripture (see Ephesians 3:1-5, 2 Peter 1:21). The apostle Peter spoke the words of Acts 2:38 before Matthew, Mark, Luke, and John wrote the words contained in their gospels. Being from regions beyond Jerusalem, most of those who heard the words of Acts 2:38 had not heard Jesus speak (see Acts 2:9-11). Even those who had heard Jesus speak failed to understand His message; therefore they crucified Him (see Acts 3:17, 1 Corinthians 2:8).

Historically, the Jews offered sacrifices with an understanding that they would invoke the forgiveness (appeasement) of God. Even on Pentecost, they believed that they needed to respond in order to receive forgiveness of God. Therefore, they asked, "What shall we do?" (see Acts 2:37). Peter had just preached a persuasive sermon designed to convince the audience that Jesus was the Christ and Lord (see Acts 2:36). Obviously, some who heard also believed, for their hearts were pricked (see Acts 2:37). Hearts are never pricked until belief comes. In addition to believing, they asked what to do. In other words, they were now asking, "After believing, what (else) shall we do?"

If they had been forgiven (saved) just by believing, Peter should have told them so. If they had been saved just by believing, Peter misled them by allowing them to believe that there was something they needed to do in order to be saved. In the past, they had killed and offered an animal in their effort to receive forgiveness of sins. Peter informed them that no longer would they have to kill a lamb. The lamb (Jesus) had already been slain. Now, they must repent and be baptized to embrace the death of Jesus. Only after Jesus had been raised from the dead did He make the connection or correlate baptism with salvation (see Mark 16:16). No wonder then that Peter relates baptism to salvation (see Acts 2:38).

But what about Romans 10:9-10? Let's set the stage.

1. Those to whom the apostle Paul addressed this letter were called and had become saints (see Romans 1:6-7).
2. They had died to sin (see Romans 6:2).
3. They had been baptized into Christ and His death (see Romans 6:3).
4. They had been raised from the dead to walk in the newness of life (see Romans 6:4).
5. They had become united with Jesus (see Romans 6:5).
6. Their old self had been crucified with Christ (see Romans 6:6).
7. They had obeyed from the heart the doctrinal teachings (see Romans 6:17).
8. They had been freed from sin (see Romans 6:18).
9. They had become servants of righteousness (see Romans 6:18).

10. Jews from Rome had been in Jerusalem on Pentecost (see Acts 2:10). It is likely they were baptized at that time.

Therefore, the apostle Paul said to the believers—those who had already been baptized—"Confess and believe" (see Romans 10:9-10).

What about Ephesians 2:8, which states, "For by grace you have been saved through faith"? The Ephesians had heard the message of truth (see Ephesians 1:13a). They had believed the message of truth (see Ephesians 1:13b). They had been baptized (see Acts 19:1-5). In Acts 8:30-32, the eunuch did not understand what he was reading from Isaiah chapter 53. Philip began at Isaiah 53:7, the place where the eunuch was reading, and preached Jesus to him (see Acts 8:35).

1. How could Philip preach Jesus when the name Jesus is not once stated in Isaiah chapter 53?

2. How could Philip demand that the eunuch believe that Jesus Christ is the Son of God when believing that Jesus Christ is the Son of God is never stated in Isaiah chapter 53?

3. How could Philip introduce the subject of baptism while preaching Jesus from Isaiah chapter 53 when baptism is not stated in Isaiah chapter 53?

4.   How did Philip understand Isaiah chapter 53
     when the eunuch did not?

The answers to all four questions are the same. Philip had a Holy Spirit-led post-resurrection understanding of the Old Testament (see Acts 6:5) and the eunuch did not. God more fully revealed His will to the apostles and prophets (see Ephesians 3:5). Philip had heard the message from the apostles in Jerusalem (see Acts 6:1-5). There are some things that had not been understood before, but came to be understood only after the resurrection of Jesus.

Because Philip had a Holy Spirit-led post-resurrection understanding of the Old Testament, God enlightened him to understand things more fully than others understood. God enlightened His apostles and prophets to understand the Old Testament. When we read the New Testament, we gain insight into the inspired minds of the apostles and prophets (see Ephesians 3:5). Jesus recognized that men needed a post-resurrection understanding of the Old Testament scriptures. Therefore, He opened their minds to understand them (see Luke 24:44-47). God opened Lydia's mind to understand (see Acts 16:14); her understanding led her to be baptized (see Acts 16:15). The Corinthians had been baptized (see Acts 18:8). Earlier, Paul alluded to their baptism (see 1 Corinthians 6:8-11). He even reminded them of the role of baptism in the deliverance of the Israelites (see 1 Corinthians 10:1-4).

Where does the Old Testament teach the purpose of baptism? It does not. It just illustrates it. The lamb's blood became available for the Israelites (see Exodus 12:21-28), yet the Israelites were not free from bondage until they passed through the sea (see Exodus 14:26-29). God saved Israel on the day that they passed through the water (see Exodus 14:30). The Holy Spirit's inspired commentary called that experience a baptism:

> For I do not want you to be unaware, brethren, that our fathers were all under the cloud, and all passed through the sea; and all were baptized into Moses in the cloud and in the sea; and all ate the same spiritual food; and all drank the same spiritual drink, for they were drinking from a spiritual rock which followed them; and the rock was Christ (1 Corinthians 10:1-4).

Scripture does provide a roadmap toward the salvation that is found only in Christ Jesus. We can ascertain the will of God through reading Scripture. Obedience to this guidance results in the best possible life on earth as well as positions us for the best possible life beyond this earth.

OTHER BOOKS BY JOHN MARSHALL

Good and Angry:
A Personal Guide to Anger Management

God, Listen! Prayers That God Always Answers
(includes an addiction-recovery guide)

The Power of the Tongue:
What You Say Is What You Get

Final Answer:
You Asked, God Answered

Success Is a God Idea

FOR MORE INFORMATION

For further information about John Marshall, his ministry,
and his ministry resources, you may contact him at:

John Marshall Enterprises
P.O. Box 159
Stone Mountain, Georgia 30086

(404) 286-1139
www.TheTeacher.us
jm@TheTeacher.us
jdm@johnmarshallenterprises.com

Printed in the United States
33391LVS00001B/32

9 780974 069371